MAN IN HIS WORLD

Also by Calvin Wells

Bones, bodies and disease

To SATRA and
to RICHARD and CATHERINE

I owe grateful thanks to my daughter, Satra, who drew the figures for this book, typed my manuscript and let me use her name as a linguistic exemplar.

Calvin Wells

MAN IN HIS WORLD

JOHN BAKER LONDON

© 1971 *Calvin Wells*

Published in 1971 by
John Baker (Publishers) Ltd
5 Royal Opera Arcade
Pall Mall London SW1

SBN 212 98383 0

*Printed in Great Britain by
Billing & Sons Ltd, Guildford and London*

CONTENTS

ILLUSTRATIONS

Plates

Drawings

1 ANTHROPOLOGY

What is it all about?

The short answer to this question is: 'Us.'

Anthropology is about us, as human beings; about everything we are and do; all the different races of mankind wherever they live, whenever they lived. It is about all the things that people make, how they behave, what they believe and what they look like. It studies man in all his myriad aspects. It tries to find out when and how he first appeared on our planet, what sorts of men roamed the world in ancient times and how they differed from us of today. It explores foreign lands and strange tribes to learn how people dress and eat, how men and women marry, how children play or witch doctors make magic. It studies the trade routes of lost civilizations and the trade unions of modern industry. Above all it asks *why* people behave in the way they do.

Nothing about the life and customs of mankind is beyond its study. That is why it is the most fascinating and thrilling of subjects. There is something in it for each of us, no matter where our interests lie. If we are inquisitive about the lives of Tibetan monks or want to know more about the meaning of pop music, anthropology will help us find the answers.

In a subject as vast as this no one can know it all.

Usually anthropologists specialize in a more or less narrow field in one of the main branches of the subject.

Human evolution tells the story of the fossil remains of ancient men and the animals – monkeys or apes – which resemble him most closely.

Physical anthropology deals with the differences between recent races. It is about their anatomy and physiology, the shape of their bodies, their different kinds of blood, their physical abilities or limitations, the features they inherit and the way they are related to one another.

Archaeology and Prehistory tell the story of the wanderings and achievements of ancient peoples before the days of written records. Great vanished cities like Mohenjo Daro of the Indus valley, long forgotten towns like Machu Picchu in the high Andes, or one tiny

flint arrowhead all have their enthralling tales to tell when once
we learn to read them.

Social and cultural anthropology probe the way in which modern
people live together, whether in primitive groups or civilized
nations. And because we shall often speak of 'primitive peoples'
we should straight away, perhaps, define what is meant by 'primitive' when applied to human populations. It is, of course, a relative
term, but it must be understood to have a purely cultural, not
anatomical or biological, significance. Primitive cultures, broadly
defined, are those (*a*) which lack writing, (*b*) have a low level of
technical achievement, (*c*) where society is organized in small
groups such as tribes or clans rather than in large cities or nations,
(*d*) where social relationships based on family and home locality
are dominant, and (*e*) where there is relatively little specialization
in work or social behaviour. These are rough and ready criteria
which must not be pressed too far or applied to all groups indiscri-
minately. Man is a social animal and these branches of the subject
deal with how people behave towards each other in the communities to which they belong.

Linguistics is the study of languages. These are always a part of
our cultural heritage and we cannot properly understand a people
and how they see the world around them unless we know their
language and the curious ways in which it expresses or modifies
their thought.

Other sub-divisions of anthropology exist. *Psychology* explores
the attitudes, motives and behaviour of persons and groups.
Ethnography collects facts about different tribes or other individual
communities. It is an essentially descriptive subject which merely
records details of what can be observed, whilst *ethnology* seeks to
analyse and explain the ethnographer's material. *Sociology* is the
science which deals with the development and nature and laws of
human society. It evolves theoretical ideas about the basic principles of social existence, it studies practical problems such as
crime, drug addiction, class differences and racial prejudice, and
it is concerned with social philosophy, with the values and ethics
and trends of human life in society. Although it deals with personal relationships, just as social anthropology does, it tends for
historical reasons to work mostly in the sphere of the complex
Western societies. The theoretical differences between social
anthropology and sociology continually grow less as each extends

its field of enquiry to overlap the other, but so far it has remained convenient for anthropologists to concentrate chiefly on primitive peoples and for sociologists to deal with contemporary civilizations. It should also be said that although some anthropologists would agree that, in theory, their subject is concerned with the total study of man, in practice no one person can achieve this and a narrower field of investigation is unavoidable. This book will certainly give greater emphasis to primitive than to advanced societies.

However, anthropology always aims to fuse many kinds of knowledge about mankind into one coherent whole. Only by doing this can we grope towards an understanding of the most wonderful, and most personal, of all epics: the splendours and miseries of human history and human hopes.

2 EVOLUTION

The emergence of man

Evolution, *Dryopithecus, Ramapithecus, Austra-lopithecus, Homo habilis*, Java and Pekin Men, Neanderthal Man, *Homo sapiens sapiens*, Stone Age industries: Palaeolithic, Mesolithic, Neolithic; the subsistence revolution, the age of metals.

Astronomers believe that the earth first took shape about three thousand million years ago. From geologists, we know that extremely simple living organisms had already appeared on it in the pre-Cambrian epoch at least a thousand million years ago. Since then ever more complicated forms of life have evolved. Here are a few of the landmarks that can be found in the fossil record of past ages.

(1) From the Silurian period (400 million years Before the Present) only fish and other forms of marine life have left their remains.

(2) Abundant land plants were present in the Carboniferous period (300 million years B.P.).

(3) Dinosaurs and other reptiles dominate the Jurassic (150 million B.P.).

(4) Small animals, including tree shrews and other Primates (the natural order to which monkeys, apes and man belong), were well established in the Eocene period (60 million B.P.).

(5) The first monkeys appear in the Oligocene deposits of the Egyptian Fayum (35 million B.P.), which was then tropical forest or open glades. The most complete of these specimens is a skull of *Aegyptopithecus zeuxis*, a kind of monkey which nevertheless had some definitely ape-like characters, especially in its teeth. It might have been ancestral to an important group of Primates, the Dryopithecines, which were common in the next geological period.

(6) This was the Miocene (25 million B.P.) and one of these creatures was *Dryopithecus africanus* of East Africa. It was the size

of a small chimpanzee but lightly built and it lacked the powerful bony crests for muscles which are seen in modern apes. It was only partly adapted to life in the trees: a semi-'brachiator' or arm swinger. Other species of this animal lived in Africa and India.

Also in India, in the Siwalik Hills, lived *Ramapithecus punjabicus*. This, and *Kenyapithecus africanus*, are the earliest known *Hominidae*, which is the zoological family to which the human species belongs. It is distinguished from the *Pongidae*, the family which includes living and extinct anthropoid apes. Both these families can be grouped into the superfamily *Hominoidea*.

Dryopithecus had U-shaped jaws with parallel sides, large canines, a cutting type of premolar tooth and a pattern of tooth wear which indicated chewing in the vertical plane. But *Ramapithecus* is nearer to the human type in having an evenly curved dental arcade, no cutting premolar, and dental attrition of a pattern which indicates lateral as well as vertical chewing. It may have been terrestrial rather than arboreal, and partly bipedal in its habits.

(7) The next geological period was the Pliocene (12 million B.P.), during which evolution of the Primates no doubt continued steadily although almost no remains of them have survived.

(8) Then, nearly three million years ago, the Pleistocene period began. This is the period of the Ice Ages. It also saw the evolution of the earliest known human beings, together with a very interesting group of creatures called the Australopithecines – a word meaning 'southern apes', although they are hominids rather than pongids (Fig. 1).

Apart from baboons, almost all the early Primates lived wholly or mostly in trees. The Australopithecines descended to the ground and their skeletons, especially the hip bones, leave no doubt that they walked nearly upright. This was an achievement of tremendous importance because it meant that their hands were now not needed for support; they could be used more or less as we use them today.

The first *Australopithecus* to be found was at Taung in Rhodesia, in 1924. Since then parts of several dozens have been discovered. They were about the size of a modern gibbon and had skulls with an average capacity of only just over 500 cubic centimetres. This

B

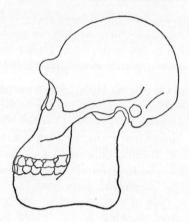

1 Profile of an Australopithecine skull.

is very close to that of gorillas but far below the range of modern man (1,000–2,000 c.c.).

Their ability to walk and sit upright must have given them a great advantage over the other animals around them. It let them peer over the tall grasses of their savannah homelands on the look-out for danger. It freed their arms and hands which could now be used for seizing carrion that more powerful beasts had killed and temporarily deserted. In this way their forearms took on the valuable function of accessory jaws and were released for the performance of fine movements.

One of the most interesting facts about the Australopithecines is that, at several sites where their fossilized bones have been found, they have been associated with crude 'pebble tools' of the Oldowan culture – the earliest of all the Stone Age industries. It is not certain that *Australopithecus* made any of these implements. It seems more probable that they were made by a very early form of true man, *Homo habilis*, who was contemporary with him, may have preyed on him and even brought about his extermination. Dr. L. S. B. Leakey, supported by an impressive group of anthro-pologists, is convinced that it was *Homo habilis* who made the tools found in the Olduvai Gorge. But this view is still not universally accepted. Uncertainty has also existed as to whether the Australo-pithecines were our direct ancestors or not. At present the trend of evidence suggests that they were more likely to have been a specialized group which became extinct after they had branched away from the main evolutionary line leading to modern man. There is some support for this from the fact that the earliest *Homo habilis* remains appear to be even more ancient than any of the Australopithecine series.

An interesting group of fossils are those from Java which used to be called *Pithecanthropus erectus* (the erect ape-man). He has now been renamed *Homo erectus*. Parts of some twenty individuals survive and they date back to about 450,000 B.C. A closely similar type, 'Pekin' man, lived just a little later. Remains of about forty of these people were found at Chou-K'ou-Tien, in China (Fig. 2). Only seven bones were from any part of their bodies except the head, which may imply that these skulls were head-hunters' trophies.

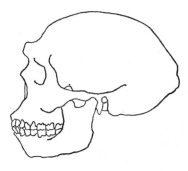

2 Profile of a *Homo erectus* skull from Chou-K'ou-Tien.

The Javan and Chou-K'ou-Tien people all had small skulls (about 850–1,050 c.c.), with flat receding foreheads, narrow frontal bones and great bony brow ridges projecting over their eye sockets. Their jaws were heavy and chinless. Like the Australopithecines, they seem to have been off-shoots from the evolutionary line, not direct ancestors of modern man.

Pekin man is important because with him we find, for the first time, clear evidence of the regular use of fire. This must have been a powerful aid to these ancient hunters. It was only with the discovery of fire that they could compete successfully with bears and tigers in occupying habitable caves. It has been suggested that the control of fire led to the development of rules against incest. For the first time it enabled small family groups to live apart from the communal band and the need for incest prohibitions developed in order to exclude sexual rivalry from within the nuclear family. This must remain uncertain but there is no doubt about the importance of fire in cooking. Human teeth and human stomachs are relatively unspecialized organs. Our teeth cannot crush the cellular walls of fibrous vegetation in the way that browsing animals such as cattle or elephants do; our stomachs cannot digest great gobbets of raw meat as the carnivores can. But cooking vegetables breaks down their cell walls, to release the sugars and proteins within, and roasted flesh is easier to digest than raw. This meant that when meals came to be cooked their *caloric* or food value became more readily available to people and the risk of starvation receded. Another effect of cooking is to soften food. This gives the jaws less work to do and allows the temporal muscles – the main chewing muscles – to become smaller. These muscles take their origin from the sides of the skull, where they exert a constricting pressure on the bones. As they become smaller the pressure is reduced and the skull can expand to accommodate a larger brain. There is some evidence that this is a continuing trend in human evolution, combined with a reduction in the size of both the upper and lower jaw.

During the Pleistocene period there were four main glaciations or Ice Ages, separated by long interglacial phases when the temperature rose to be considerably warmer than it is today. During the last of these interglaciations a species of man, which had begun to develop even before the third Ice Age, greatly extended its range. This species was formerly called *Homo neanderthalensis*, or Neandertal man, but is now included in our own species *Homo sapiens* as a separate subspecies *Homo sapiens neanderthalensis*.

He was a great evolutionary advance on the old Javan and Chou-K'ou-Tien types, with their various cousins in Europe and Africa, such as the Heidelberg and Atlanthropus people – which is indicated by the modern tendency to classify him as *sapiens*. Some of the Neandertal men had large beetling brow ridges over deep eyes, and a long face which jutted out rather like a muzzle, with a heavy, chinless jaw. Their teeth were big and had large spaces inside them, a condition known as *taurodontism*. They were rather shorter than most Englishmen or Americans today but stood fully upright. Their skulls are interesting because, although they had

3 (*Left*) A Mousterian flint point from Northern France. Length 4¾ in.
4 (*Right*) A Mousterian flint scraper from Northern France. Length 4¼ in.

low receding foreheads, they were not small skulls. The average Neandertal brain was bigger than ours today.

These men had evolved a complicated culture, the *Mousterian* industry, and made excellent stone tools including ones with triangular points, side scrapers and end scrapers (Figs. 3 and 4). No doubt they were skilled woodworkers, too. They probably made clothes to keep out the cold because they survived long into the last Ice Age, and some of them seem to have lived quite close to the glaciers in what must have been extremely severe conditions. They often made their homes in overhanging rock shelters where their hearths and tools remain as evidence of their passing. Men of the Mousterian culture, or their flint tools, have been found over a huge area from central Asia to the Channel Islands and from Germany to North Africa. It should be emphasized that they varied greatly in physical appearance – especially the numerous ones from Central and Eastern Europe. A few of them from a cave in Palestine seem half-way towards modern man and it is possible that they may actually have interbred with modern types. But they seem mostly to represent another of the divergent lines of evolution: a specialized form branching away from the main stream leading towards modern man.

It appears that these people, many of whom would surely have seemed physically crude and primitive to us, had already deve-

loped some sort of belief in an after-life. Mousterian burials have
been found in which the corpse had been covered with red ochre
and supplied with simple grave goods, presumably for the comfort
of the dead person in a world to come. It may be that we today
owe a far greater debt to the spiritual beliefs of Neanderthal man
than we have so far begun to imagine.

The fourth and last Ice Age was broken by several short remis-
sions when the great cold eased somewhat. But before it finally
ended Neanderthal man had become extinct, unless a handful of
scattered survivors lingered on. A few late descendants of them,
physically crude and highly specialized types, have been recognized
at the African sites of Florisbad, Saldanha and Broken Hill
(Plate I). But these people were, indeed, blind alleys of human
evolution.

Before the last glaciation was over a new type of man had
appeared and dominated the earth. This was *Homo sapiens sapiens*,
the species to which we ourselves belong and the only one now
living.

Homo sapiens sapiens – modern man – has existed in the form of
several different stocks or races. One of the first was the famous
Cro-Magnon race, named after a site in the Dordogne region of
France (Fig. 5). It was men of this type who followed closely on
the heels of the Neanderthalers and who probably played a large
part in their disappearance.

The Cro-Magnon men were quite unlike their predecessors.

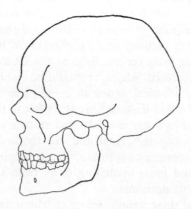

5 Profile of a Cro-Magnon (*Homo sapiens sapiens*) skull.

They were tallish and well built. They had skulls with high rising foreheads and no beetling brow ridges. Their mandibles had fully projecting chins. Above all, they had evolved a much more elaborate culture and were soon to produce some of the most wonderful flint tools ever to be made.

The first important cultures to be produced by these new men were the *Châtelperronian* (Fig. 6) and *Aurignacian* industries, though the roots of both had been foreshadowed long before. The typical implement of the Châtelperronians was a flint knife with one straight, razor-like edge and a curved blunted back to it. In western Europe the Aurignacian industry was supplanted by the *Gravettian* which came in from the east. All these industries made bone, as well as flint, tools and these included pins, borers and spear tips.

The various peoples who made these tools hunted reindeer and bison but in western Europe horses were an even more important quarry. Below the great plateau cliff of Solutré in east central France it is estimated that the remains of a hundred thousand horses lie buried. They were driven over the brink by the Aurignacian horse hunters and provided a rich source of meat, hide and bones for tools. Further east vast numbers of mammoths were hunted, probably by stampeding the herds and trapping them in pitfalls. The mammoths provided ivory as well as meat, and occasionally their larger bones were even used in building huts.

During Gravettian times a beautiful flint industry was evolved. This was the *Solutrean*, named after the famous village of Solutré. These tools now included elegant spear points and the so-called 'laurel leaf' blades (Fig. 7). The finest of them might be more than a foot long and no more than a quarter of an inch thick.

About this time the weather began again to get colder and coinciding with this another culture evolved: the *Magdalenian*. Not surprisingly, in view of the cold climate in which it developed, the material culture of the Magdalenians resembled in some ways that of the Eskimo. As well as excellent stone implements, they made many objects in bone, ivory and antler (Fig. 9; Fig. 10). These included barbed fish spears and harpoons, fish-hooks, hammers, chisels, sewing needles and toggles for clothing.

These Upper Palaeolithic peoples were the wonderful cave artists whose work is so well known. It was Aurignacians who painted the great hunting scenes at Lascaux; Magdalenians who

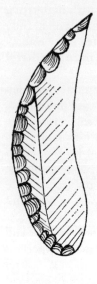

6 (*Left*) A micro-Châtelperronian
flint blade. Length 1⅛ in.

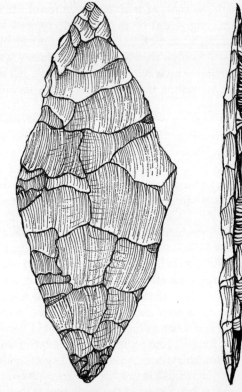

7 A Solutrean 'laurel leaf' flint blade.
    Length 4½ in.

8 (*Left*) A Late Magdalenian 'pointe foliacée'
from Laugerie-Basse, France. Length 2⅝ in.

put the bison on the Altamira cave, as well as leaving clay models of these animals at Tuc d'Audoubert in Ariège.

Throughout this period when the Ice Ages were drawing to a close, migrations of peoples or spread of their industries were taking place continuously over vast areas of Europe, Asia and Africa, soon to be followed by the first invasion into the New World, about 17,000 B.C., over the ice bridge of the Bering Sea. Many varieties of these cultures are known. It would be too con-

10 A Magdalenian bone harpoon head.

9 A horse's head carved in reindeer antler from Mas d'Azil, France.

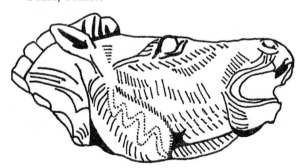

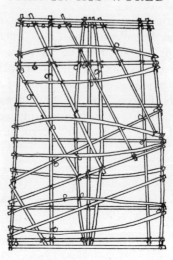

11 A navigator's chart from the Marshall Islands. Shells are attached
to a cane-work frame to show the relative position of various islands.

fusing to describe them here but it must always be borne in mind
that they existed. A brief description of a few of the European
industries gives a woefully incomplete picture of the real extent of
these upheavals and little idea of the complexity of many of the
industries which had evolved. By this time most of the Old World
at least, was seething with population movements of this kind.
Such is the restlessness of man that, even with primitive equipment, he remains undaunted by hundreds of miles of open sea.
Figure 11 shows a navigator's chart of the kind used by the Marshall Islanders and other argonauts of the Pacific in their great
voyages across Oceania to Easter Island and the coast of South
America. At what period men first added some sort of sea travel
to their ancient land trekking is unknown. Nor can we do more
than guess what kinds of rafts, tree trunks or boats provided their
earliest water transport.

More or less coinciding with the end of the last Ice Age was the
end of the Palaeolithic period – the Old Stone Age.

It was succeeded by the *Mesolithic* or *Middle Stone Age*. During
this period, as far as Europe is concerned, a group of important
cultures evolved. They were all distinguished by the presence of
tiny flints, called *microliths*, which may be only a few millimetres

12 Mesolithic flint microliths. Lengths ¾ in.

across (Fig. 12). Perhaps some of the smallest were glued into wood to make the earliest hack-saws or barbed spears (Fig. 13).

Several of these cultures existed at the same time but they were concentrated in different types of country.

The *Maglemosian* industry was based on forests and the rivers or marshy lakes within them. Fishing and fowling were important here, and trees, for dug-out canoes, were felled with large hafted axes. The people of the *Azilian* culture, who have left many curiously painted pebbles to perplex us (Fig. 14), were often located round river mouths. The *Tardenoisians*, who seem to have been the first people to domesticate dogs, lived mostly in regions of open heath or scrubland. The *Obanian* and the *Ertebølle* cultures were more or less limited to shore lines where their distinctive 'kitchen middens' (great mounds of mollusc shells) are characteristic.

Again, similar cultural developments were taking place over many parts of Asia and Africa and by now were well afoot in the Americas.

It was during the Mesolithic period, about 6,000 B.C., that Britain became separated from the continent by a southerly extension of the North Sea across the lower reaches of the river Rhine. Before that happened the Rhine had flowed through what

13 One probable way in which microliths were used.

14 Painted pebbles of the Azilian culture.

is now the English county of Norfolk where the forests on its banks had once been the haunt of bears, lions, elephants, rhinoceros, beavers and zebra.

The next phase of man's material development was the *Neolithic* or *New Stone Age.*

It was a period of unparalleled importance in the evolution of human culture because it ushered in what is called the *subsistence revolution.* This simply means that for the first time in a million or more years people began to produce food instead of just gathering or hunting it. Food production was due to the invention of agriculture, with ways to grow crops, and pastoralism, with its techniques of herding and stock-raising.

It is hardly possible to overestimate the importance of the Neolithic food revolution. It meant that people now had to stay more or less in one place, because having sown a crop they had to be there to reap it. For the first time they were confronted with a need for really sturdy buildings: when a crop has been reaped it must be stored to keep it dry and as safe as possible from rats and mice (Fig. 15). This led to a demand for well-built granaries, which in turn inspired the building of better and more permanent houses than any that had been made before. Stores of barley and wheat created a need for better cooking and domestic utensils, as

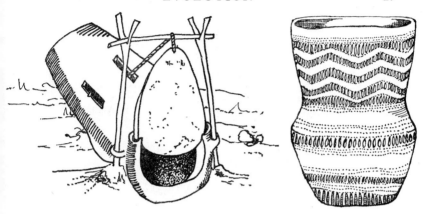

15 (*Left*) A mousetrap from Mundigak, Baluchistan. 3rd millennium
B.C. (After B. de Cardi.)
16 (*Right*) A pottery vessel of the 'Beaker culture'. Height 5¾ in. From
Denton, Lincs.

a result of which pottery was invented (Fig. 16). As long as people
had been semi-nomadic hunters and gatherers large, heavy
earthenware jars would have been impossible to carry around,
whilst small ones would have been of little use.

This revolutionary innovation seems first to have taken place in
the oasis of Jericho about 9,000–8,000 B.C. From there it spread
rapidly throughout the Near East and eventually by steady diffusion along the migration and trade routes to all parts of Europe and
throughout most of Africa and Asia. With it, profound changes
took place in the structure of society: food-gathering patterns gave
place to those associated with food production. What these were
will be discussed in the chapter on Human Geography.

In spite of these outstanding advances we must remember that,
as their name implies, the Neolithic peoples still used stone tools
(Fig. 17), not metal. Their method of making these implements
was, however, an improvement on how it had been done before,
but they still used types such as microliths and 'laurel leaf' blades
which had been evolved in earlier periods. They were the first to
grind and polish their tools, many of which were drilled for hafting
on wooden handles as mattocks or adzes (Fig. 18). In modern
experiments these stone axes have been used to fell tall pine trees
in a few minutes.

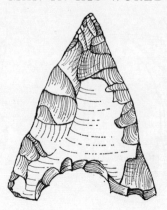

17 A Neolithic flint arrowhead.

With the Palaeolithic domestication of fire and the Neolithic invention of agriculture and pastoralism, man had taken the two most revolutionary and progressive steps in the whole of his long history. By combining the power of furnaces with the increased leisure offered by a food-producing way of life he next learnt how

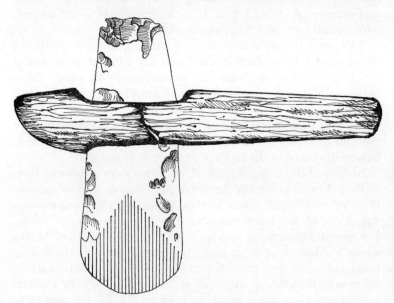

18 A Neolithic flint axe, polished and hafted. Length of blade 12½ in.

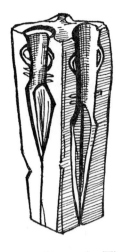

19 A four-sided stone mould for casting spear
heads. Bronze Age, Lough Gur, Ireland.
Length 6¾ in.

20 A Bronze Age socketed sickle.
Length 5 in.

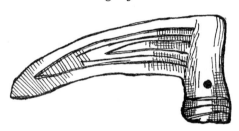

to smelt metals. This new technological advance ushered in first
the *Bronze Age* and then the *Iron Age*. Bronze, an alloy of copper
and tin, came first because it was the easier to manage. It was
developed, about 3,000 B.C., by the farming folk of the Near East
at a time when the peoples of western Europe were still Mesolithic
hunters and fishers, unless the recent excavation of Lepenski Vir
in Yugoslavia makes it necessary to change the accepted history of
civilization. This seems to suggest that relatively high civilized
living had already been reached there by 5,000 B.C. Bronze makes
excellent tools or weapons (Fig. 19). Sickles, axes, knives, arrow-
heads, bowls, swords and many other objects survive from
hundreds of Bronze Age sites (Fig. 20).

After the domestication of sheep, woollen clothing had been
introduced to supplement the ancient use of hide or skins which
may have dated back a hundred thousand years or much more. In
the peat bog burials of Denmark the bodies of men and women
who died three thousand years ago have been preserved, together
with the garments in which they were buried. At Egtved a Bronze
Age girl was found wearing a jumper with a round neckline and
half-length sleeves. She also had a corded mini-skirt held up by a
belt with a great circular clasp in front of her slender waist. Her
hair, worn off her forehead, hung loosely about her shoulders.
Plate II is an exact copy of her attire. This, with evidence from
other burials and from statuettes, shows how close these ancient
fashions were to the pullovers and mini-skirts of today.

The change from tools of copper or bronze to those made of the more efficient iron was an inevitable and rapid development as soon as the craft of metallurgy had improved its techniques. But the use of metals, though of great importance, did not in itself constitute such an outstanding revolution in man's cultural life as the production of food a few centuries earlier or the command of fire half a million years before that. Only two technological advances have so far rivalled the previous two: the invention of printing from movable type, and of powered machinery with the internal combustion engine.

At this point, then, we may leave the evolution of man. He began as a creature hardly to be distinguished from other species of Primates and with no more cultural ability than theirs. As he evolved physically and mentally his technical achievements grew. By Middle Palaeolithic times he was already a subspecies of *Homo sapiens*, as we are another, though he had not yet attained to more than a Mousterian culture. A few thousand years later he invented the processes of agriculture and after ten thousand years more he had devised machines that will work almost indefinitely as long as they are supplied with fuel, together with computers, antibiotics, nuclear fission and the scientific method. That, to the present, is the story of his biological and technological evolution. We can only surmise what his future may be as atomic energy is harnessed to his service and the corridors of the galaxy open to his space-craft.

3 RACE

How people differ physically

Caucasoids, Negroids, Mongoloids, other subdivisions of race, blood groups, genes, mutation, natural selection, genetic drift, hybridization, race, language and culture, intelligence and racism.

A *race* is a group of people who possess a distinctive set of physical features which they have acquired as a result of biological inheritance (Fig. 21). This definition of race, applied to humans, is roughly equivalent to what we would call a 'breed' when applied to domestic animals. The difference is that whereas, by careful selection over many generations, we can get an almost pure breed of canaries or cattle, all races of men are extremely *hybrid* or mongrel . . . though many persons resent being told so.

Many different physical features have been used to separate the population of the world into its racial groups. Skin colour, hair texture, shape of head or of nose, height, projection of jaws and types of blood group are a few of these. The difficulty is that these traits are not just 'present or absent' features in which one can make a clear-cut decision. 'White' skin (it never really is white) and 'black' skin (nor is it ever truly black) would be easy enough to separate. Unfortunately everybody lies somewhere on a gradient between the two, ranging from a pinky gold or a very pale olive biscuit, through light and medium brown, to a deep chocolate. Hair ranges all the way from lankly straight to corkscrew frizzy; noses from narrowly hooked to wide and snub.

Despite these difficulties anthropologists have managed to reach broadly similar conclusions even when they use different methods of classification. Nevertheless, differences of opinion are bound to arise and we cannot do more here than have a look at one possible view.

Before considering what human races are identifiable it must be said that some races resemble each other much more closely than others. We can, then, group the ones that have most in common into large *stocks* or varieties, as the great naturalist Linnaeus was the first to do in the middle of the eighteenth century.

C

The three major stocks are: the *Caucasoid* (sometimes called the 'Europoid') or white stock; the *Negroid* or black; and the *Mongoloid* or yellow stock.

21 Four racial types as seen by an ancient Egyptian. From a sketch in the tomb of Sety I at Thebes. XIX Dynasty, about 1300 B.C.

The Caucasoid races are (*a*) the *Nordic*: which contains a high proportion of tall, fair, wavy-haired, blue-eyed, narrow-nosed and long-headed people; (b) the *Alpine*: tallish, fair and wavy-haired but with broad heads; (c) the *Mediterranean*: of medium height, olive to light brown skins, wavy hair, narrow heads and noses; and (*d*) the *Hindu*: fairly tall, brown skins, variable noses and narrow heads.

The Negroid races are (*a*) the *African negroes*: mostly tending to be tall, with narrow heads, broad noses, projecting jaws, everted lips, woolly hair and dark brown skin; (b) the *Oceanic* or *Melanesian negroes*: similar but shorter and some with aquiline noses; and (c) *Negritoes* (the pygmy races): similar but extremely short and many with broad heads.

The Mongoloid races are (*a*) the *Asiatic mongoloids*: who are mostly below average height, with light brown or yellow skins, medium noses, broad heads, straight dark hair and the 'slanting' or 'Mongolian' eye – which is really a fold of the upper lid over the nasal corner of the lower; (b) the *Malaysians*: similar but with darker skins and lacking the Mongolian eye; (c) the *Amerindians*: tall to medium, with variable head shapes, broad face and nose, otherwise similar. (The hook-nosed, 'hatchet-faced' Indian of popular fiction is a rare variant.)

A few other races can be recognized that do not fit into these three major stocks. They include the *Polynesians* of Oceania, the *Australoids* of Australia and the *Veddoids* of India and the East Indies. The *Ainu* of Japan, the hairiest people in the world, and the *Bushmen* of the Kalahari desert seem to be partly related to the Caucasoids and Negroids respectively. They are probably the last dwindling remnants of races that were once widely spread.

Figure 22 is an attempt to show how these stocks and races can be grouped together. There is nothing immutable about this classification; it is merely a convenient one which appears to reflect with fair accuracy what is found when the varieties of mankind are observed. Other classifications exist using different terminology and slight shifts of emphasis.

Most people know that it is dangerous to take blood out of one person and transfuse it into another without taking care to find out whether the two lots of blood can safely be mixed. This is because there are different types of human blood, some of which are not compatible with others. These different types, which are geneti-

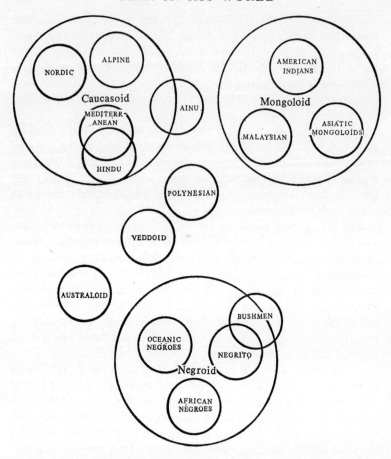

22 A diagram of the relationship of human races. Their distance apart represents their degree of relationship. (After Kroeber.)

cally determined, are called blood groups. There are several dozens of them.

Blood groups help to distinguish between races or smaller populations for two reasons. Firstly, the frequency with which the various groups occur differs from one community of people to another. Secondly, unlike hair, skin, stature or nose shape, there is no overlap between them: a person is either group MN or not; group O or not.

The first blood groups to be discovered were the ABO system, in which persons may be of four main types: AB, A, B and O. In England their frequencies are roughly: AB 2 per cent, A 43 per cent, B 7 per cent and O 46 per cent. In central Asia the combined frequency of the AB and B groups is very high, reaching more than 40 per cent in many populations. This is a clear racial difference but it may imply more than that. It is possible that in Stone Age times the gene which produces the B groups was absent from Western Europe. And there is some evidence that it was introduced to the west by migrating bands from the east in Bronze Age times, later to be reinforced by the invading hordes of Attila in the fifth century and further augmented by Tamerlaine's invasions in the fourteenth.

The Amerindians have exceptionally high O frequencies, some populations reaching 100 per cent for this blood group. Figure 23 indicates the way in which transfusions can be given in the ABO system. The arrows show directions in which blood transfusions may be safely given.

In the MN system similar differences are found. The three

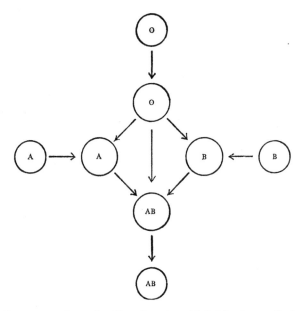

23 A diagram to show the directions in which blood transfusions may be safely given within the ABO system.

possible groups and their approximate average world frequencies are MN 50 per cent, M 30 per cent and N 20 per cent. Australoids are exceptional in having gene frequencies for N of more than 80 per cent, whilst some Eskimo have up to 90 per cent M.

Another system, the Rhesus or Rh groups, is also extremely useful in distinguishing between populations.

In the nucleus of plant or animal cells which are actively dividing, small microscopic rods are found which are called *chromosomes*. Their number varies from species to species; in human beings there are forty-six, of which twenty-three come from each parent. On these chromosomes are a large number of biochemical structures which, because they have been derived from the two parents, are present in the growing seed or ovum from the moment of fertilization. These are *genes* and each one has the power to influence the development or functioning of the individual organism in some specific way. Features such as hair texture, eye colour, blood groups and innumerable other characters, many of which are used to distinguish between racial groups, are inherited traits whose form is 'genetically' determined by these structures.

During the course of evolution races can originate in four ways:

(1) By *gene mutation*. This is a sudden change in a gene that makes it produce a different behaviour or appearance in the future from what it has done in the past.

Almost every known animal can make Vitamin C (ascorbic acid) in its own body, whether or not it gets any from its diet. As a result, these animals never suffer from the Vitamin C deficiency disease *scurvy*. The only animals that can get scurvy are man, monkeys, guinea pigs, an Indian fruit bat and a subtropical bird, the red vented bulbul. This presumably means that somewhere back in the ancestral tree of each of these species an independent mutation occurred in the gene which had previously enabled them to make ascorbic acid, as all other animals do.

It is gene mutation which produces the bleeding disease *haemophilia* from time to time in families hitherto free from it. The only way a new gene can increase its frequency of occurrence in a 'gene pool' or population is either to increase its mutation rate or to have a higher selective advantage than the original form. Because most living organisms are the product of long millennia of evolutionary selection and adjustment to their environment, most new mutations do more harm than good. They are what the geneticist refers to as 'lethals' or 'semi-lethals'. Occasionally a mutation occurs which gives improved survival value and it is these that tend to persist. The accumulation of different characters as a result of differing gene mutations may eventually lead to two races evolving from what was originally one homogeneous group.

(2) By *natural selection*. This means that genes which produce variations having survival value in some particular environment will be likely to establish themselves in the population that lives there, thus producing a race adapted to the locality. Where hot tropical climates encourage the wearing of few clothes, the skin is likely to be exposed to intense sunlight. This can cause serious damage unless it is protected by an abundance of pigment. Almost all races living in hot countries have a lot of the dark pigment *melanin* in their skins.

(3) By *genetic drift*. Throughout his evolution man has always been a restless migrant and wanderer. If a small band of people split off from a larger group and set up a fresh settlement at the end of some long migration it is very probable that their genetic composition will not be the same, on average, as that of the population they have left. A gene with an average frequency of 20 per cent in the parent group may, by pure chance, occur in 35 per cent of the emigrants, another gene with a 5 or even 10 per cent frequency in the home group may not be represented at all among the scanty band of wanderers. The gene pool of the new population and their descendants differs, therefore, from the ancestral group: it has 'drifted' away from that of their forebears. The racial character of the original and the new communities will henceforth be different. It is probable that some of the peculiar traits of the Bushmen can be explained in this way, and the Amerindians may have lost an original B antigen gene by the same process in the course of their long migration from the 'high B' areas of Asia.

(4) By *hybridization*. This is the formation of new races by cross-breeding between earlier ones. All human populations owe most of their features to this process.

It is, unfortunately, extremely common to hear people talk about 'the French race' or 'the Bantu race', sometimes even 'the Middle Minoan race'. This should never be done. A race is a biological fact determined solely by anatomical or physiological characters. It is wrong and confusing to apply the term in any other way. France is a country, a fact of geography and politics; its people are a nation which includes Caucasoids, Negroids and Mongoloids among its members. Bantu, like Aryan, is a name for a family of languages. Middle Minoan describes a culture, a way of life. If we want to talk about the people we ought to refer to 'the French', or 'Bantu Speakers' or 'bearers of the Middle Minoan culture' and avoid ambiguity. This is another way of saying that race, language and culture are independent of each other. People of the African negroid or Asiatic mongoloid races may speak Bantu, Aryan, Sinitic, Semitic or other languages and practise primitive tribal, advanced Western European or traditional Chinese cultures.

It is often assumed or said that some races are 'lower' than others. People who assert this do not always mean the same thing. They may intend us to believe that their so-called 'lower' races have inferior brains or intelligence; or that they are in some mysterious way of less moral or 'spiritual' worth. Sometimes they only mean that these alleged 'lower' races have simpler cultures than others, although, as we have just seen, race and culture are independent of each other.

Whatever the propagandists of this doctrine have in mind it can be firmly said that such beliefs are false. To act upon them is always stupid and often vicious. These theories are usually put forward by politically arrogant nations or party groups who want to justify themselves in the eyes of the world for the persecution of another group whom they wish to oppress or exterminate. The revolting treatment of Jews by the German Nazi party will long remain an unparalleled example of these pernicious doctrines of *racism*.

It is true that peoples of different tribes, ethnic groups and races differ greatly in their cultural achievements. But differences of culture are the result of many chance happenings, of historical accidents and the accumulation of technological innovations. A primitive culture does not imply primitive intelligence. Indeed, it could be argued that to survive as Eskimos do, amidst the rigours of the Arctic, or as Bushmen do, in the Kalahari desert, requires a high level of intelligence.

As far as anatomy is concerned, there is no reason to suppose that

genes which produce blue eyes, fair skins and narrow noses are
'superior' to genes which produce brown eyes, dark skins and
broad noses, although the end results may be better adapted to
some environments than others. Caucasoids, with their thin lips
and extensive body hair, are more like the simians in these features
than Negroes are; whereas Negroes are closer to simians in skin
colour and nose breadth. Brain size is no criterion for a value
judgement. Pygmies and Australian aborigines, as well as many
Negroid groups, average a rather smaller brain than that of the
Caucasoids, but Eskimo and some Negroids average larger brains,
as the Neanderthals did. Variations of physiology and function
show no overall genetic superiority or inferiority, although differences in adaptation to environment are again common.

Far more important, because more charged with emotional
tension, is the question whether real differences in intelligence and
moral qualities exist between races. Morality may be disregarded
here because in normal people it is wholly conditioned by cultural
not genetic factors. As for intelligence, it can be firmly said that
no clear evidence of racial inferiority has ever been proved in any
people. It is true that many intelligence tests have been applied,
especially in the U.S.A., to Negro and non-Negro groups, to
'whites' and to Chinese, and in the past many of these tests have
been interpreted to suggest white superiority. On careful scrutiny
it is always found that something about these tests has been heavily
weighted in favour of the Caucasoids. The other groups have been
handicapped by emotional maladjustment, poor social background,
lack of previous education, language problems or different attitudes towards the test. Everything we learn from the study of
racial psychology reinforces the view that variations in behaviour
and achievement are due to cultural, not genetic, differences.

The United Nations Educational, Scientific and Cultural Organization (Unesco) sums up the position when it says: 'Available
scientific knowledge provides no basis for believing that the groups
of mankind differ in their innate capacity for intellectual and
emotional development.' We are all brothers under the skin.

4 CULTURE

The richness of human life

Definition, cultural relativity, culture and
society, culture change, inheritance of culture,
selection, organization and function, sub-
cultures, status and role, basic personality,
institutions, culture and environment, integration, culture complexes, acculturation.

Culture is a word that is constantly used by anthropologists. We
need, therefore, to understand what it means, especially as its
meaning is not the same as in everyday speech.

The famous English anthropologist, E. B. Tylor, wrote: 'Culture or civilization is that complex whole which includes knowledge, belief, art, morals, law, customs and any other capabilities
and habits acquired by man as a member of society.' He meant
by this that culture is all the skills, beliefs and behaviour that we
learn from people around us, from our parents and other elders,
from our friends and workmates, from all the persons who form
the *society* in which we are brought up and who surround us in
our daily lives.

Culture is what we learn, consciously or unconsciously, from
other people. It is especially the accumulated knowledge and
integrated patterns of behaviour that are handed down from one
generation to the next.

In recent years much theorizing has been devoted to defining
culture and, therefore, what it is that we do in fact study. Some
regard it only as an abstraction, with no real existence outside the
mind of the anthropologist, but this ignores Einstein's opinion that
'The belief in an external world independent of the perceiving
subject is the basis of all natural science'. A difficulty is that
psychology is the study of behaviour . . . and this might seem to
rob the cultural anthropologist of his subject. One attempt to
resolve the conflict is based on how identical objects, actions or
ideas are viewed. If we consider how a stone axe, a clan, a burial
ritual or a hunting technique is related to human beings as such,
this is a psychological approach. If we consider how axes, clans,
rituals and techniques are related to other similar or different items

independent of human involvement, this is a cultural approach. The distinction will not be laboured here. For decades anthropologists have, in practice, studied objects, customs and ideas without being unduly worried whether they were psychologists or 'culturologists' at any particular moment.

With this in mind we may be content to define culture as *the whole of social inheritance*. It is not instinctive or genetically predetermined.

All groups of people have their own cultures, some of which are very different from our own and cannot be understood in terms with which we are familiar. It follows, therefore, that we must not judge them by our own standards; we must constantly bear in mind what has been called the *principle of cultural relativity*. This means that human behaviour in any one culture can be understood and evaluated only in terms of the basic assumptions and values which that culture itself adopts. Greed, generosity, sexual freedom, habits of violence, self-assertion or meekness are qualities which have a certain significance and meaning in our culture. They are subject to value judgements and are foci of strong emotional feeling. When we meet these same qualities in peoples of other cultures we must set aside our own assumptions about them and try to evaluate them in terms of their significance in their own culture. We should assess the moral behaviour of people in other cultures in the light of what *they* have learned to accept as right or wrong, permitted or forbidden. Every object and every pattern of behaviour is in some way related to the practical and emotional needs of the people who possess it. Anthropology tries to see each item (what is called a culture 'trait' or 'element') in its context: to understand its function in the total cultural pattern and its full meaning in the lives of the people concerned. This approach, though only occasionally mentioned, must be understood as implicit throughout this book.

Now let us look at some of the qualities that distinguish culture.

The first is inherent in the definitions of it that we have already given: there can be no culture without society. We learn all the separate items of our native culture because, and only because, we live in a social group with our fellow men and women, preserving the traditions of our ancestors and adding our own small quota to what we have learned from them. We cannot imagine a culture without a society of people to practise it. On the other hand societies can exist in nature which have no culture: bees and ants are social insects whose activities are the result not of learned behaviour but of instinctive reactions.

Cultures are always changing. A colony of ants or bees presumably behaves now, by instinct, precisely as a colony of ants or bees behaved in the time of Henry VIII or William the Conqueror or Julius Caesar. But the culture of people today is very different from that of Tudor England, Norman France or ancient Rome. This is a way of saying that cultures evolve historically which is, itself, a consequence of transmission from one generation to the next. Indeed, this change in the pattern of cultures down the centuries has led to the use of convenient labels to describe them. So we speak of the culture of Baroque Germany or of Renaissance Italy; the 'Migration period' culture of the Vikings; the culture of Periclean Athens, of the Shepherd Kings of Egypt or the prehistoric 'Basketmakers' of North America.

The rate at which cultures change varies from place to place and in different ages. It was very slow throughout the three thousand years of dynastic Egypt; incredibly slow through the hundreds of thousands of years of the Lower Palaeolithic period. Today cultures are almost everywhere changing rapidly and may show extensive transformations even in one person's lifetime. In earlier times, when cultures were more static, the longer a man lived the more he could absorb from his background. He thus came to have an advantage, in accumulated knowledge and experience, over younger men who had had less time to learn than he. Because of this the old man was probably valued for his wisdom and know-how, just as he still is in some primitive societies where change has taken place relatively slowly. But among cultures which change quickly, an old man – conditioned to the pattern in which he grew up – may find himself at a disadvantage. He is now in a world that is largely new and strange to him. His youthful experience gives him little help in his altered circumstances and, lacking the adaptability of young people, he finds himself 'left on the shelf'.

Although all cultures change in time, the shift is always more or less gradual. Even the cultures of Victorian England or of Colonial America glided almost imperceptibly into the Edwardian and Republican periods.

In the same way cultures shade into one another geographically.

A great gulf separates English culture from that of the Eskimo, the Bushmen of South Africa or the Semang of the Malaysian forests. But our French neighbours have a culture very like ours, despite a few striking differences (such as language) and many minor ones (such as eating habits and currency). As we follow changing patterns of culture across Europe and Asia, through Germany, Poland, Russia, Turkey, Persia and India to Korea, we gradually find greater differences from our own, even though none is as remote from us as Eskimo or Bushman. In general, cultures differ from each other in proportion to their distance apart. But here generalization is likely to confuse rather than illuminate. In comparing two separate societies, their many cultural elements do not all differ from one another to the same degree. Some traits may be rather alike in the two groups, others quite dissimilar. Our patterns of housing, feeding and religion are utterly different from those of the Eskimo, but our method of classifying family and kindred is almost identical with theirs. The clan and kinship organization of most Bantu African groups is quite unlike anything we have. Their language is totally different, so are their religion and traditional dress. But it happens that in the functioning of their legal systems they are, broadly speaking, fairly close to us.

Cultures owe much more to their inheritance than to their own originality and inventions. This applies to even the most rapidly changing ones. Our basic diet and habits at table; our social behaviour and attitudes, the language we talk, the mythology and religion we believe in; the way we clothe ourselves, our work, our amusements, even our gestures are almost all acquired from the accumulated cultural storehouse of past generations. We make minor changes (and it may be difficult to adjust even to these) but our many modern inventions such as zip-fasteners or television still represent only a small percentage of our total cultural wealth. This is seldom recognized. We like to think of ourselves as wholly original and inventive. But most of the basic elements of our culture are not only old, they have filtered through to us from many far off places (Fig. 24). Wheat was first domesticated in the Near East, so too were cattle, though we easily forget this when we eat our bread and roast beef. Potatoes, tomatoes, and tobacco were originally cultivated by the American Indians, coffee in Abyssinia, tea in China. Sheep were first domesticated and their wool woven into cloth in the Near East; the complicated process of producing

24 On the right is an Ancient British coin, a gold stater. On the left is the Greek model from which it was derived by the intermediate steps which are shown between them.

silk was evolved in China; felt was invented by Asiatic nomads – but who thinks of the hordes of Attila when he puts his trilby hat on? Rubber, including rain-proof cloaks and balls for play, was first used by the natives of Central America. Soap was invented in ancient Gaul; writing was first devised by the Egyptians, printing in Renaissance Germany, paper in China.

Cultures are selective in what they absorb from other peoples. When two cultures come into contact they start to blend with one another. The classical Greeks absorbed some elements of their culture from Egypt, some from Crete and others, such as the alphabet, most of their astronomy and their system of weights, from Asia. Recent Japanese culture derived its idea of a god-emperor from ancient native sources, its writing and philosophy from the Chinese, Buddhism from India, car production, penicillin and television from the West. But despite this massive and eager absorption of foreign cultural elements, certain features of the alien culture are likely to be rejected. The ancient Greeks never adopted the Egyptian habit of mummification because it conflicted with their religion and their basic attitude towards the human body. The Japanese, whilst taking a great deal from China, rejected foot binding as incompatible with their aesthetic concepts. They also rejected the Chinese system of competitive examinations for admission to the civil service and important posts in the court or government because this system would have clashed with their feudal society in which high office was the prerogative of birth or influence, not merit.

These last three examples show the organization of culture in action. Because of certain basic attitudes that pervaded Greek and Japanese society, the traits mentioned here were rejected. They could only conflict, not harmonize, with the existing cultural system. The potential variety of human behaviour is immense. No single society could possibly practise all the diverse traits that are known. Their multiplicity would lead to chaos through unpredictability, whilst many patterns of behaviour would be mutually contradictory. Hence the *imperative of selection* is forced upon every society. It is an over-riding essential if life is to be bearable and tolerably predictable. And always when recording what elements are or are not found in any culture, we should ask the same questions: What is the *functional significance* of each item? How do the different traits combine with each other into a smoothly integrated system which functions to satisfy the basic biological, psychological and social needs felt by all humans and human groups. If we approach exotic societies in this way we soon find that the various elements in their cultures have been selected in accordance with certain dominant values and assumptions which they have about the nature of man and the cosmos, of good and evil. In this way a coherent and harmonious pattern is established.

Many other examples of cultural selection might be given. Insurance is still difficult to sell to some Moslems because it is felt to conflict with the Koranic prohibition against gambling. Either it is or it is not the will of Allah that your house shall be burned down: to insure 'lest it might be' is a gamble and an impiety. The English have taken from America a great mass of culture elements (Coca-Cola, mormonism, movies, chewing-gum) but we have rejected baseball and the electrocution of criminals. The French have accepted football and the week-end from us whilst remaining uninterested in tea and cricket. Even on our very doorstep the English, whilst borrowing tartans, whisky and porridge from the Scots, have little use for bagpipe or haggis.

It is not always possible to say why, or even whether, some items of an alien culture are accepted and others rejected. It may be especially difficult to decide in the case of intangible traits. Has England been influenced by certain American attitudes to divorce? What is the effect, if any, of South African apartheid attitudes on the behaviour of the French towards their non-Caucasoid minority groups?

Some anthropologists have developed the concept of *sub-cultures*. By this they mean that different groups of people within a single society have their own distinctive cultural pattern. To define these different groups they abstract, in a more or less arbitrary way, categories of persons such as men and women, old or young, rich or poor, bankers or carpenters. This concept is of only limited use because the selected categories are seldom as clear cut as the male-female one and the arbitrary choice can be pushed to absurd limits. In a sense all families, even all individuals, have their own distinct sub-culture in so far as everyone has personal uniqueness of thoughts, behaviour, attitudes or ability. More important is the fact that in stressing these 'sub-cultures' we are likely, by fragmenting the picture, to lose sight of our main aim – the synthesis of cultural elements into a meaningful whole. It is, of course, true that certain broad categories of persons think and behave differently within any one cultural system, and as long as we see them as parts of a total pattern it is useful to contrast group differences.

This is true even in the most primitive tribes where there is little specialization of work and where the material content of their lives has never advanced beyond a Stone Age simplicity. It is vastly more apparent in the huge and complex cultures of modern industrial civilizations. Under these conditions none of us can begin to know or to practise more than a small part of the great culture amid which we have grown up.

But a more fruitful and dynamic approach is to think in terms of roles. Each person in a society has his own *status*, which may be defined as his position in the overall pattern. A role is the dynamic aspect of a status. It is how a person behaves *because* of what he is. Role and status are inseparable. Thus we may more rewardingly say that men and women have different roles in the total culture, so have the old and the young, the skilled and the unskilled. Our role determines the part we play in any social situation. It especially fixes our position and status relative to other people and so may be described as a distance-setting mechanism. The Tuareg of the Sahara are a locally endogamous people who reckon descent bilaterally and have various patterns of after-marriage residence. This introduces some ambivalence into their social relations in and outside their kin group. Tuareg men cover their faces with a veil almost all the time, including meals. The custom seems to serve as a method of maintaining a generalized social distance from other people, a distance which can be made more specific by fine adjustments to the veil's position. They lower it slightly when at ease with a group of companions, raise it close to eye level in the presence of a father-in-law or other senior relative by marriage.

Some elements of culture will be practised by every normal member of the society: with us, wearing clothes, using spoons and sleeping under cover are of this kind. Traits such as these are called *universals*. But all cultures allow a fairly wide choice about what is normal behaviour. A Cheyenne Indian on the warpath could choose whether to carry a bow and arrow, a spear or a club. We can choose whether to wear a hat, a cap or go bareheaded; whether to be Anglicans, Methodists or Catholics; to play rugger, soccer, bridge or billiards; and much else. Traits such as these are called *alternatives*. The stability and cohesion of any society depend to some extent on the relative proportion of universals to alternatives in its culture. Many of these alternatives are especially prominent in setting the so-called 'sub-cultures' apart from one another. With this in mind, let us look at some of the ways in which the total culture of our society can be broken down into smaller areas.

In no society, however primitive, do men and women do exactly the same things. Even among peoples who survive without any kind of agriculture, simply by gathering their food from the country around them, the men will probably do most of the hunting whilst the women pick fruit or berries and dig up roots (Plate III). This is because women, when they have young babies to look after, cannot move about so widely and quickly as the men. As they stay nearer home, the women in many societies do most of the house chores, cooking, making clothes and often tending the gardens, too. The men, who hunt, will almost certainly make the weapons and will often be specialists in heavy work such as building canoes, felling trees to make clearings in the forest and building houses whenever these are large.

In most tribes, as also amongst the advanced industrial cultures, men and women wear different clothes and ornaments, though sometimes the distinctions here are very slight.

D

In our own society men and women perform very different roles, although less so now than in Victorian times. Today women still do most of the housework such as cooking, dusting, sewing and knitting. They take a less active part in most professions, even in medicine where their influence is important. Few women are engineers; in factories of heavy industry they are chiefly restricted to office and canteen work; and there is almost no place for them in the church. (In this we differ greatly from the Ifugao of the Philippine Islands, where the priesthood is almost entirely in the hands of women.)

Despite certain modern tendencies towards an overlap between the sexes they still dress differently most of the time, do their hair differently, smoke differently (how many women use a pipe?), walk and sit differently and even use different forms of speech. All these are, of course, cultural or 'sub-cultural' differences which help to reveal, though they are not the cause of, differences in role.

In all societies young people have different interests from the middle aged and the middle aged have interests and activities that are not the same as those of the elderly. In our modern English culture this may make the young and the old feel they have little in common – although, in fact, their common cultural ground is immense.

Nevertheless, young people are apt to show certain cultural traits little practised by the elderly: they like pop music, mini- or maxi-skirts and other special styles of dress; they value restless mobility as shown by their passion for driving around in cars or on motor bikes; they read books of the James Bond type; in social relationships they are likely to be casual and intense by turns. They are concerned mostly with the present and the immediate future. Elderly people, by contrast, show cultural features little valued, or even despised, by the young. They dislike noise and prefer to remain at home; they probably have more interest in housework and gardening. They tend to be backward-looking and lament that 'times are not as good as they used to be'. They often wear long underpants. Their choice of reading, music, hair-style, topics of conversation and even food may be very unlike that of teenagers. Individual exceptions are found but the general tendency holds good.

These differences exist in primitive tribes as well as among complex societies, and again we may express this as being a difference in the roles of the young or the elderly.

Young Kikuyu of East Africa do not belong to the secret clubs that are so important to their elders. Among the Comanche, a buffalo-hunting tribe of the Great Plains of North America, young men had the role of warriors. They were expected to behave in a vigorous, aggressive way, never overlooking an affront and always seeking to dominate their companions. If they lived to become elders of the tribe their role changed. They were then expected to be peace-loving, gentle, slow to take offence and willing to forgive slights or abuse. This change in the cultural behaviour which was demanded of them as they grew from youth to age was one that many of them found very difficult to achieve. It required a profound change in what we call their basic personality.

But in spite of many variations we can say that in nearly all societies people over the age of about forty-five are mostly concerned with preserving the old-established elements of their culture. It is the people under thirty-five who are more interested in pressing new reforms or innovations.

The above mention of *basic personality* calls for some elaboration, by way of parenthesis, because it is an important concept in anthropology. It postulates that the way in which children are treated and brought up, from earliest infancy, will play a dominant part in the way they react to their parents and in their attitudes to other kinsmen and to society in general. Societies differ greatly in the way they treat small children. So when the children grow to adulthood their reactions will, in turn, be different from one society to another. It is these various attitudes and behaviours, formed as a result of culturally standardized patterns of upbringing, that constitute the basic personality structure. Its importance is that the basic personal attitudes which prevail in a society will, in turn, influence the development of the political, religious, economic, artistic and other features of its culture. Here, then, is a true two-way interrelation: child-care customs mould basic personality and the basic personality patterns are later carried over into a wider area to mould the culture. This is a dynamic concept of great significance. It shows that people are not merely passive receptors of their culture, they work emotionally on what they receive and project various responses towards it. Or, to put this another way, it shows how basic personality integrates with, and serves to integrate, the many social and cultural systems that we find around the world.

The children of Alor, an island of Indonesia, though wanted, are neglected. Their mothers work hard in the fields and pay little attention to feeding or fondling the infants. When a baby bawls, an older child or some casual adult eventually stuffs some half-chewed banana in its mouth, but no attempt is made to relieve its emotional tension or satisfy its hunger for love and security. Later it is teased and mocked and given no help whilst it learns to walk or play. Adults deliberately make it jealous; they promise food to the child but spitefully withhold it. As a result, the basic personality of the Alorese is anxious, suspicious and lacks interest in the outside world, which is felt to offer no security. Enterprise has been inhibited. These people are filled with repressed hatreds and aggressions which they dare express only furtively. They have little ability to co-operate because they are always on guard against the hostility of neighbours. Social cohesion is barely achieved through attitudes of dominance and submission, not through affection and mutual trust. Their religious art is careless and slipshod – which projects towards the ancestor gods their feeling about parents. Their warfare was an affair of stealthy and cowardly forays, with vengeful attacks on women and children as well as men. It was a continuation of their childish tantrums into adult life. Relations between husbands and wives are bitter and distrustful. In this manner Alorese child-handling shapes a basic personality which later shapes the culture.

In spite of the precision with which some psychologists describe this process of personality formation we should guard against accepting the theory uncritically. We must not assume that a similar result could not be achieved by different means.

Even when two persons are of the same sex and age much of their cultural behaviour may be strongly dissimilar if they belong to different classes of the population. The middle classes have a set of values, behaviour and interests different from those of the aristocracy or the lowest orders of the society.

There are often great differences between the 'sub-cultures' of people whose work takes them into widely separate areas of experience. A coal miner has skills and interests, not only when he is working down a pit, that are very different from those of a bricklayer, a garbage collector, a financier, an actor, or a circus clown. Occupational differences in culture include many aspects of life. A sailor, a farmer and a physician, for instance, though sharing English as a common language will have separate working vocabularies that may comprise hundreds of words and expressions that are unkown to each other. They read different books, dress and eat differently, choose different friends or amusements, and have different legal obligations and rights.

The blacksmiths in a tribe of Bedawin camel breeders have a range of culture that contrasts vividly with the rest of their group. They are often foreigners who marry only among themselves. They make swords, spears and utensils but take no part in the fighting and raids that are common between these desert bands. If their property is accidentally stolen by a raiding party it will usually be returned through the good offices of the smiths in the hostile group. They have more freedom to move from one tribe to another than the rest of the camel breeders.

But once again the essential aspect to recognize is not the separateness of farmers and physicians, of Bedawin and black-smiths, but their overlap and integration. They all have inter-locking roles and statuses in the great cultural web of their society. A weakness of this 'sub-culture' concept is that it blurs the significance of functioning groups of persons who act together despite their many personal differences – functioning groups which are called *institutions* and which are the effective basis of cultural activity. A banking house is such an institution: it needs young clerks of both sexes, older executives, highly skilled financial advisors, messengers and cleaners of more restricted education, telephonists, maintenance staff, legal advisors and overseas representatives. Only by considering their combined functions will the significance of the total institution be understandable.

Little reflection is needed to reveal that cultures are closely integrated with the environment in which each society lives. A people can only adopt a pattern of culture that is compatible with the physical conditions of their background, though their relationship to the environment is always a reciprocal one. Environment partly determines the sort of culture and society they have but is itself subject to cultural modification. The material cultures of the arctic Eskimo, Polynesian atoll dwellers, jungle tribes of Amazonia, and the aborigines of Central Australia have little in common because the natural background of each is so distinct that almost no overlap can occur. The Boro forest dwellers cannot build igloos, Eskimo cannot grow yams, the Arunta of Australia cannot fish for sharks.

Only with the inventions of Western civilization can modern man largely ignore his physical background by creating an artificial environment. He cools his tropical house by air-conditioning, generates electricity to heat and light his arctic dwelling and makes himself independent of the limitations of local agriculture by eating canned foods from all parts of the world.

But very different cultural elements and patterns often exist side by side in almost identical environments and it is an especially interesting, though extremely difficult, task of anthropology to account for this. We can show that these diverse patterns of culture serve to satisfy the needs of the societies in which they are found but we cannot say, historically, why one system rather than another has been adopted. It is not clear, for example, *why* decorative art patterns of the American Plains are strongly geometric

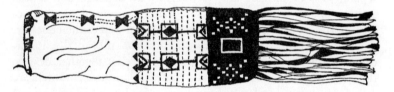

25 Geometric ornamentation on a Plains Indian pipe and tobacco bag. Sioux tribe. (After Goldenweiser.)

26 Curvaceous pattern on birch bark. Penobscot Indians. (After Wissler.)

(Fig. 25) whereas further to the north-east, in the areas of birch-
bark canoes and caribou hunting – amongst the Penobscot and
Naskapi Indians – they are mostly curvilinear (Fig. 26). Nor can
we say why the Crow reckoned descent through the mother and
the Omaha through the father.

We have already referred several times to the fact that distinct
culture traits integrate with each other to form functional patterns
of activity and interest. This is sufficiently important to merit
further illustrations. If we consider the element *television* in our
own culture we can see that it is not something isolated in one
corner of our sitting-room. Wires connect it physically to a supply
of electricity and hence it is dependent on the electrical supply
industry as a whole. It has links with the acting profession of those
who appear on it, with the educational, religious, musical and
other backgrounds of its many programmes. It is used for official
government announcements, for propaganda and for broadcasting
news. It is integrated with the economic system of the country
and with various industries, since many sets are made for export
as well as home sale, and it plays an incalculable part in advertising
many other kinds of goods. Our own financial position is involved
with it because we have to find the money to buy or hire it. It has
legal connections since we need a license to install one, and com-
ments made on it might give rise to actions for slander. It modifies
our eating habits, our family and social life, our conversation.
Even our health, mental or physical, may be influenced by it.

A consequence of this close integration between television and
other elements of our culture is that it could not be abolished
without having profound effects on all of them. This is what is
really meant when we say that culture has integration as well as
content. One element cannot be changed or deleted without up-
setting others, as was dramatically shown in 1918 when the
eighteenth amendment to the U.S.A. constitution was passed.
This was the Act that introduced the prohibition on drinking
alcohol. Its sponsors simply wanted to stop drunkenness by
removing one solitary element – alcohol – from the total cultural
content of the nation.

The result was catastrophic. Illicit manufacture at once began;
illegal channels of supply were found; respectable citizens turned
law-breakers; the police and even judges were corrupted by
bribery; family unity was often divided by different attitudes to

the new law; political antagonisms were made worse; economic chaos prevailed in many industries which were concerned with drink; severe health hazards developed because people began to drink poisonous substitutes for good whisky or wine.

Enthusiastic missionaries, who used to try to reform practices they did not like, often caused distressing upsets in well-integrated primitive tribes. They could do this merely by seeking to abolish a single culture trait that appeared to them to be immoral or contrary to Christian belief: polygyny, bride price and female circumcision are examples. The disruption and misery which followed these well-meaning efforts clearly reveal that cultural traits such as these are never single elements in isolation. They infiltrate into innumerable aspects of the natives' life.

When a group of integrated culture elements is found clustered together in a fairly defined geographical region it is sometimes spoken of as a *culture complex*. The concept has some limited use as a descriptive term. Examples are: the great maize-growing complex of the Mexican Indians or the reindeer complex of the Lapps, on which the basic food economy of these peoples depended. Medieval Europe was dominated by a culture complex focused on the church. The arts, crafts and literature; men's conduct and beliefs; the legal and political set-up of the continent; its wars and its alliances were to a great extent the result of this ecclesiastically based complex.

The Eskimo have a culture complex associated with whales. We have several. There is one, for instance, associated with the pop music, pop groups, discs, hair-styles, clothes and much else in our teen-age sub-culture. Culture complexes are really centres of predominant interest for any group on which wide areas of their activities are focused. Many also show the organization of culture in its most dynamic aspect, but care must be taken not to mistake the merely accidental coming together of traits (known as *adhesion*) for a true functional association.

Culture organization is well shown in the cattle complex of the Pakot, a Nandi-speaking tribe of Kenya who number about 40,000. They are herders of cattle, goats and sheep and cultivators of sorghum, eleusine and other crops by slash-and-burn rain-weather farming. Their chief interest is cattle and most of their activity involves these animals. They have an elaborate vocabulary to describe them and the men, who mostly control the herds, regard them as objects of beauty – especially a kind of steer called *kamar*, which they decorate with bells, compose songs about and 'initiate' through a sacrificial feast. Wealth is reckoned in terms of cattle, goats and occasionally land. One steer is worth about fifteen goats. When the young men are initiated into adulthood by the *sapana* ceremony, a steer is slaughtered and eaten as part of the ritual. Similar feasts are held for other important ceremonies such as *eghpadia*, the ritual purification of a warrior; *mis*, a peace talk with neighbouring tribes; *kikatat*, praying for a sick man; *kinta*, a funeral feast, and *achula*, given by a man who has committed adultery, as part of his fine. Milk and ritual meat are highly esteemed foods with sacred qualities; there is a taboo against eating them on the same day. At a wedding, the bride is anointed with milk, honey and manure. Cattle are regarded as objects of affection; their ownership confers prestige and they are the chief form of bridewealth to validate a marriage. In the economic life of the Pakot, cows are regarded as a form of productive capital. They, and steers, are also used in an elaborate form of trade called *tilia*, which consists in an exchange partnership between two men who are not clansmen. This trading relationship develops various overtones. Partners exchange gifts, support each other in disputes and develop ties of intimacy.

It is easy to see that the Pakot 'cattle complex' is organized into every aspect of life through their basic assumptions about what is good and evil, sacred or profane. Cattle validate marriage and initiation ceremonies, consecrate magico-religious rituals, are the basis of wealth, status and economic activities, serve to pay legal fines and compensation, are objects of aesthetic delight, emotional attachment and never-ending discussion. Moreover, the ritual feasts and their occasional less formal slaughter provide an essential part of Pakot subsistence diet. Cattle are the great cohesive matrix of Pakot society: deprived of them their culture would disintegrate.

We can end this brief review by glancing at the impact of our modern Western culture on the cultures of primitive groups. This is seen wherever Europeans irrupt into hitherto undisturbed tribes, and are followed by a diffusion of traits from one group to the other, which is always heavily loaded against the tribal society. It is only within the past few years that some of the peoples of central New Guinea have come under pressure from white civilizations. The primitive group shows a process of culture change which leads it increasingly to conform with the patterns of the dominant society. This process of drastic alteration in its original culture is called *acculturation*.

A common story is for the primitives to abandon much or most of their former pattern of living and to become, in effect, a lowly sub-caste within the complexities of the Western culture, whilst retaining their identity. The exchange of a few traits between the cultures which are in contact is not enough to produce acculturation. This happens only when the invading settlers extensively disorganize the economic basis of the natives' life, together with their social structure, religious system and other values. If not exterminated they become wage labourers performing a few simple or special tasks. They may be hired as pearl divers, gardeners, house servants or grooms. In New Guinea a few have been trained as police.

Great differences exist in the ability of these traditional cultures to resist being swamped or obliterated by the Europeans. The Samoans and the Maori have retained much of their old culture pattern. They have also absorbed a great deal from the whites and have integrated it with their own pattern of living. As a result, their societies still continue to flourish. In the south-west of the U.S.A. the Navajo have firmly preserved their cultural identity, whilst the neighbouring Apache have almost lost theirs. The Bushmen of the Kalahari have little resistance. They retreat before the pressure not only of whites but also of the surrounding Bantu-speaking tribes.

Jungle dwellers of Amazonia seem exceptionally sensitive to white infiltration. Several careful estimations of tribal numbers are available for this area and they all tell the same story. A population of about 1,000 Sabane in 1926 had fallen to 21 by 1938; 10,000 Nambikwara in 1916 are said to be now reduced to a few hundred, although there are differences of opinion about this; the Munducurús fell from 20,000 in 1915 to about 1,200 in 1950.

The dying out of many groups is not only, or perhaps often, due primarily to the 'fragility' of their cultures. Diseases, such as measles and tuberculosis, or deliberate killing, have been even more commonly the cause. There is evidence that Brazilian jungle tribes are still being exterminated by smallpox which is spread from gifts of clothing deliberately contaminated with the virus.

An article in *Current Anthropology* recently estimated the population of the Western Hemisphere when Columbus made his landfall as 100,000,000 people. In less than two centuries after their first contacts with Europeans 95 per cent had disappeared. It seems likely that these figures are an exaggeration, but even if they can be reduced by as much as three-quarters it can fairly be said that the discovery of America by the Old World is the most catastrophic tragedy ever to have afflicted any branch of the human race.

5 HUMAN GEOGRAPHY

Human Geography and how people get food

Semang, Eskimo, Bushmen, 'North-west Coast'
cultures, Witotoan tribes, Tikopia, Tungus,
Yoruba.

All over the world people, whether they live in primitive tribes or
advanced civilizations, like to enjoy their leisure hours in dancing,
carving statues, singing songs, embellishing their houses, watching
plays, making bead necklaces or fancy hair combs, playing games
and many other pastimes.

Man's capacity to feel boredom, his inventive mind and the
restless itching of his fingers seem always and everywhere to impel
him to further activity when his working day is done. But before
he can sit down to model even a simple clay doll or carve patterns
on a drinking gourd he must put one task firmly behind him: he
must ensure that he has enough to eat.

From the dawn of human history – indeed from the dawn of
life, perhaps a thousand million years ago – every living creature
has been faced with the choice: 'Eat or die.' Plants get their food
through their roots, bacteria absorb it across their cell walls,
higher animals suck, peck or gnaw from their environment
whatever they need to keep them alive.

If the people in them are to survive, every tribe and every great
city must somehow come to terms with the world around it and
wring from its environment enough food for the body's needs. To
this rule there can be no exception. Sooner or later any man or
any group of people who cannot eat must die. Those of us who
live in towns (which is where most Europeans and North Americans
do live) can easily forget this. We are so used to seeing a constant
supply of food in shops, restaurants or our larders that we tend
to take it for granted and give no thought to how it came there.

It is interesting, therefore, to see how different peoples have
solved this basic problem of survival. No other animal – not the
dog, nor the rat, nor even the flea – has been able to live in so
many different places as man. Only man inhabits the whole surface
of the earth. As a result of this he has had to learn ways of winning

food from a bewildering variety of environments: sun-baked deserts, polar ice sheets, coral islands, tropical forests, high mountain ranges, marshes, tundra, and even the slums of sprawling cities.

At the most primitive level, presumably at the level of mesolithic or even palaeolithic man, the food quest consists of nothing more elaborate than picking berries, grubbing roots, catching a few animals or gathering any scraps of carrion left by more powerful predators. Peoples whose economy is near this level can be described as *Simple Food Gatherers*. Their patterns of survival are strikingly various but the stark poverty of their environment or their limited ability to exploit it give them many features in common. A brief glance at a few of these groups will illustrate this.

THE SEMANG

Projecting down from the mainland of eastern Asia is a long tongue of land: the Malay peninsula. Its tip lies almost on the equator and its interior is a region of dense tropical jungle in the depths of which live the Semang. These are a group of *negritoes* (pygmies of a strongly negroid type). They roam through the forest in parties which seldom number more than a couple of dozen individuals, most of whom belong to a single family group.

They live by gathering fruits or berries, digging up roots, and hunting. Although the forest is dense, the game and the edible fruits are sparse so the little band has to keep moving throughout most of the day. They shun large animals such as tigers and leopards, but the men hunt wild pigs, rats, monkeys and birds. They kill these by shooting with arrows which are tipped with *ipoh* poison, a preparation which may be quickly lethal to small animals. The women dig up wild yams and, helped by the children, gather berries, nuts and edible leaves.

Each of these family groups has its own territory which it shares in common. Their resources are so meagre that they never accumulate any real property. Their dwellings are nothing more than simple windbreaks of various sizes, leafed and crudely thatched to provide shelter in wet or stormy weather. Almost their only furnishing is a low couch of twigs and leaves, to raise them from the sodden forest floor at night. The Semang cannot store or preserve food and their brief leisure gives them little time to

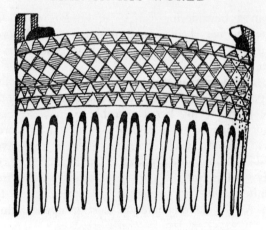

27 A Semang bamboo comb.

make elaborate articles of any kind. Each person privately owns his scanty bark-cloth clothing, his bow and fish spear, her bamboo comb (Fig. 27) and ornaments, and the bamboo tubes in which she cooks the family's food. There is almost no other personal property except *durian* trees which are owned by individuals who pass them on to their children. The fruits they bear, which smell of rotting corpses, are a valuable and much-prized source of food.

In this primitive setting no class differences can develop, no individuals amass a surfeit of goods, no great chiefs rise to power. The simple affairs of daily life are carried out by mutual agreement under the direction, when necessary, of some elder of the group who is respected for his common sense or ability as a hunter.

THE ESKIMO

All along the great stretch of Arctic territory from Greenland to Alaska live some of the most interesting people to be found anywhere in the world: the Eskimo. They are a short, stocky Mongoloid group who everywhere speak closely related dialects and have evolved over many centuries a way of life that is superbly adapted to their harsh environment (Fig. 28).

Today, many Eskimo groups have close contacts with white civilization and, in times of difficulty, the Canadian or United

States Governments keep a fatherly eye on them. But others still live in their old traditional way (Plate IV). Its pattern varies greatly across their wide territory and we will describe only what happens in the most typical central region from Coronation Gulf to Baffin Island.

When the snow melts in summer the Eskimo begin to hunt the herds of caribou which roam across the tundra feeding on lichen, moss and small bushes. The hunters shoot them with arrows, ambush them in narrow valleys, or drive them on to lakes covered with thin ice. When enough caribou are on the ice it breaks and the Eskimo paddle their kayaks among them, spearing them as they swim. Wolves, fish and birds are also trapped or snared by the men whilst the women and children collect berries and look after the affairs of the camp which may consist of as few as thirty persons or as many as three hundred.

The caribou not only provide food for the Eskimo: their hides are sewn into carefully tailored clothing and used to make tents; their antlers are shaped into a variety of tools; their fat can be used for fuel.

In the autumn, hunting usually ceases for a few weeks. The Eskimo gather together for festivals at which they sing songs and enjoy any stores of food they have been able to accumulate during the summer months. Then, as winter falls and the sea freezes, the camp breaks up and small family bands scatter over the ice where they will remain until the next spring.

On the ice the pattern of their life changes abruptly. Most things connected with the caribou become tabooed and they now concentrate on hunting seals. This is done through holes in the

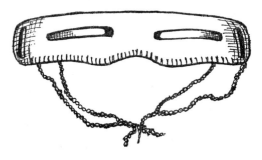

28 Eskimo snow goggles.

ice to which the seal must come to breathe. When the animal's muzzle appears, the waiting Eskimo plunges a harpoon into it. This harpoon has a detachable head to which a long hide line is fastened. As the seal plunges away the hunter 'plays' it on the end of the line until it becomes tired enough for him to drag back to the hole. In the spring, seals may be stalked and speared as they lie basking in the sunshine with their new-born young. This is much easier than waiting at their breathing holes but it can be practised only during a few weeks. The seal is an extremely important animal for the Eskimo as it provides food for him and his dogs, skins to cover his kayak, blubber for heating and lighting, hide thongs for harness and sledge making, sinew for sewing, bone for tool making, sheets of gut to serve as windows in the igloo, and much else. Even its blood is smeared on the runners of the sledges to make them glide more easily.

Polar bears are also caught, and whales are hunted from large open boats called *umiaks*.

Eskimo live during the winter in round snow houses called igloos. These have ledges inside to serve as beds, well padded with moss and furs, and small 'cubby holes' are hollowed out to store clothing or other belongings in. The whole igloo may be lined with a tent suspended from the roof by toggles. This helps to keep them warm and cosy whilst reducing to a minimum the thawing of the inside walls.

Only the men hunt seals but the women are kept busy all day preparing the kill for the many uses to which it is put. If a woman has a small baby to look after she carries it around on her back in a kind of haversack called a *parka*.

As soon as the ice begins to melt in the spring the Eskimo leave their igloos and return to the shore in readiness to begin once again the caribou hunt which marks the summer season.

THE BUSHMEN

The most barren and inhospitable area in the whole of southern Africa is the Kalahari desert. It is a region of scanty rainfall which can support little but a thin covering of grass, scrub, and stunted trees. Through this sweltering land herds of antelope and ostrich graze and when they die hyenas and vultures compete to devour the carcases.

In this wilderness live the Bushmen. They are a small, almost pygmy, race with slightly negroid faces, wrinkled yellow-brown skins, tightly curled 'peppercorn' hair, and fat, protruding buttocks (Plate v).

They live in small bands which move from place to place throughout the year as they follow the moving game herds on which they depend for food. The most important need for beasts and men alike is to find permanent water holes. In the dry winter season these are few and widely scattered, so the Bushmen hunters gather round them and shoot with arrows the animals which flock there to assuage their thirst. The arrows are tipped with various poisons but none are very effective, so the chase may last for many miles before the animal is killed. In the wet season herds of antelope can be driven into the slippery mud-flats which surround the water holes and when they are bogged down in the mire are easily speared. Snares, pitfalls and ambushes between long funnel-shaped fences are also used. Some Bushmen groups expertly disguise themselves in imitation of various animals.

The women and children add to the food – and water – supply by collecting wild melons and other succulent plants, together with berries, roots, insects, lizards and ostrich eggs. Digging sticks and roughly shaped stones serve for most of these tasks. The empty eggshells are used as water bottles (Plate VI) and pieces of them are carved to make the flat beads which are their best-known ornaments. These beads are also used for barter: they are exchanged with neighbouring Bantu-speaking tribes for tobacco, metal tools and occasional supplies of grain.

Bushman clothing is scanty. Most go bare-foot, though some groups make tough hide sandals. The men wear a loin-cloth and light cloak, the women a small apron and a large cloak or *kaross*. It serves both as a garment and as a kind of satchel or bag into which they stow melons, tortoises, firewood and much else, including their babies.

These brief descriptions of three simple food-gathering peoples, the Semang, the Eskimo and the Bushmen show how widely contrasting their environments are. They show, too, how each of these peoples had to solve the basic problem of survival in very different ways. But in spite of these differences we can recognize many similarities amongst the three groups:

E

(*a*) In each of them the bands normally comprise only two or three dozen persons – often closely related families.

(*b*) Most of the hunting is done by the men while the women and children gather berries, roots and insects, and also attend to the chores of the camp.

(*c*) They are seldom permanently settled: they are nomadic with the seasons (Eskimo) or even from day to day (Semang).

(*d*) They produce so little which is surplus to their needs that no wealth can be stored up and no person can accumulate much more than his neighbours.

(*e*) Therefore personal property is almost limited to clothing, weapons, cooking utensils, and ornaments.

(*f*) Differences in social class within the community are negligible: there can be no place for kings, princes or slaves where every man must work equally to support his family.

(*g*) Apart from the different tasks allotted to the two sexes there is little specialization within the band. All the men follow nearly identical pursuits, so also do the women. Shamans, magico-religious specialists, are prominent in some Eskimo groups but even they are only part-time operators.

(*h*) The territories in which each band hunts, fishes or gathers vegetable food are usually communally owned by the group. Produce of the hunt or scavenge may be privately owned but is often shared in common – especially in times of famine. Occasional exchanges of goods occur but there can be no substantial trade nor any need of money.

All these are features of what have been called *Simple Food Gathering societies*. They are found in many parts of the world and result from methods of food collection which rarely, if ever, produce more than the slenderest surplus above the basic minimum needed for survival. Peoples living at this simple economic level do not practise agriculture. Nor do they keep domesticated animals, except for dogs.

The 'North-West Coast' Tribes

Along the north-west Pacific coast of North America, stretching from Alaska to Vancouver Island, there lived a remarkable collection of tribes which included the Tlingit, Tshimshin, Haida, Kwakiutl and Nootka. Their traditional way of life was highly distinctive but unfortunately it also proved to be very fragile and rapidly collapsed under pressure from white Americans at the end of the nineteenth century. Although the natives themselves still survive, little is left of their culture.

These peoples lived in an area rather like the west coast of Norway. Close to the shoreline rise the rocky mountains from which many swift rivers fall, opening into fjords before they flow out to the sea. Off shore innumerable islands provide shelter from the open ocean, fishing beaches, seal landfalls, berry-picking grounds, and canoe harbours.

The tribes living here did not *produce* any food. Like the Semang, Eskimo and Bushmen they lived only by 'gathering' – which, of course, includes hunting and fishing as well as collecting fruits, nuts, roots, shellfish and many other titbits. But unlike the three groups just mentioned, these peoples had an abundance of food, a fact which profoundly modified the pattern of their lives.

The basis of their livelihood was fishing. Every year vast shoals of salmon ascended the rivers, where they could be easily caught in nets or traps. Any that were not immediately needed for food were dried and smoked for future use. In addition, off-shore fishing provided an inexhaustible supply of cod, candlefish, halibut, seals and sea otters, whilst from the land berries, roots and occasionally such animals as bears and elk gave variety to their rich diet.

No other pure food collectors were ever able to draw on such abundance.

Because this surplus was available these tribes have been described as *Advanced Food Gathering societies*. Compared with the *Simple Food Gatherers* they show some important differences in the basic pattern of their society:

(*a*) Populations were much denser, with villages of up to 2,000 persons.

(*b*) Although slight seasonal nomadism was found, only a small number of persons took part in it. Many remained behind in the permanent villages with their large strongly-built houses.

(c) Specialization was more marked. Some people concentrated on making canoes, others wove blankets, built houses, or carved elaborate boxes and totem poles out of cedar trees.

(d) Wealth was unequally distributed and extensive personal property was owned. This included houses, canoes, furs, fishing rights, beaches and hunting grounds.

(e) Distinctions of rank were well developed so that these tribes included chiefs, nobles, commoners and slaves.

(f) In association with this they had a rich ceremonial life. Many kinds of fraternities or clubs, with elaborate rituals, were a feature of their social activities.

(g) Extensive trade occurred up and down the coast and, to help this, clam and other shells were used as money.

(h) Small war parties, often travelling in fleets of canoes, were organized in the autumn, and many of the slaves were captured during these expeditions.

It is clear, therefore, that the rich food supply enjoyed by these tribes enabled them to build up a much more complicated and varied culture than was possible for peoples at the level of the Bushmen or Semang.

The Witotoan Tribes

These comprise the Witoto, Boro, Resigero, Andoke and several other tribes who inhabit the tropical forest of Brazil, near the headwaters of the river Amazon.

They live by practising simple agriculture supplemented by hunting and gathering wild plants. Their chief crop is manioc, from the tubers of which they prepare a kind of flour called *cassava*. Because the manioc contains prussic acid the preparation of the cassava is a complicated task (Fig. 29). They also grow yams, sweet potatoes, different kinds of gourds or squashes, beans, maize, plantains, pawpaws and pineapples.

We may say, parenthetically, here that maize, beans and

29 Squeezing manioc in a 'stocking' of plaited fibre to extract the prussic acid.

squashes have been called the 'triumvirate' that formed the basis of American Indian agriculture and hence of society. Symbolically, maize was most important because it was upon this plant that a vast amount of ritual was focused in many parts of the continent. It is a spectacular plant to behold and it has been offered as the material foundation upon which the magnificent achievements of the Pueblo, Maya and Inca high cultures were based. Its defect is that it is almost pure carbohydrate, whereas beans are a rich source of protein. Cultural development is closely linked to the amount of energy available to a society and it is likely that the energy obtainable from the relatively well-balanced diet of bean protein, plus carbohydrate, was the real basis of the American high cultures. To Amazonian jungle dwellers, however, there is no question of a diet rich in surplus calories.

The Boro live in small communities of fifty to a hundred and fifty persons. A single leaf-thatched house, with a sloping gabled roof about 30 feet high, shelters the entire group. The interior is divided into family compartments, where hammocks are slung around individual fires. Their equipment consists of a few split-log stools, fire fans, palm-leaf brooms and some cooking pots. Hollowed tree trunks are hung in the roof to serve as bees' nests.

Around the house is a clearing in the forest. They make this clearing by burning off the trees and undergrowth; this, and other scattered patches in the surrounding jungle, provide the gardens for their various crops. After four or five years the soil becomes exhausted, the house starts to crumble, and the whole group moves off to a fresh site where it begins once more the heavy task of clearing the forest and building another communal dwelling.

To work their log-littered, weed-ridden clearing demands strenuous labour which is mostly done by women. They have few tools except wooden digging sticks and, very rarely, a stone axe or mattock. With this poor equipment little surplus can be produced.

The men procure small amounts of much needed meat by killing sloths, tapirs, armadillos, agoutis, parrots and monkeys. They do this chiefly by shooting them with poisoned darts from a blow-pipe which they use with great skill. The famous poison curare was an invention of the Amazonian Indians, who were the most competent poison makers of all primitive peoples, although the Witotoan were not the most accomplished among them. For all but the largest animals death sometimes occurred in a few seconds. The bow is not used, but some of these tribes use hunting dogs and poisoned spears in the chase of large game. Some tribes are said to make nets 6 feet high and up to 1,000 feet long for catching deer and peccaries. Fish, too, are caught by poisoning streams above artificially constructed weirs. They also make ingenious traps in which they catch anything from rats to jaguars (Fig. 30). Honey, larvae and a variety of fruits are gathered.

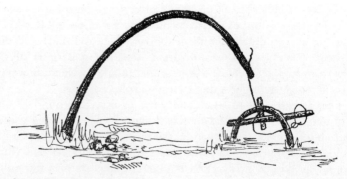

30 A spring trap. Cubeo tribe, north-west Amazonia. (After Koch-Grünberg.)

They practise a few simple crafts such as making crude pottery, carving wooden bowls, basket-making, plaiting fibre mats and knotting hammocks to sleep in, but the overall standard of their material life is very low, although it is undoubtedly an advance on that of the Semang or Bushmen (Fig. 31). They wear almost no clothes but like to paint themselves with elaborate designs and to display ornaments of shells, beads and feathers. Nose and ear plugs are worn and they pluck their beards and eyebrows with a kind of sticky gum.

31 Wooden stool in the form of an animal. Mehinacu tribe, Xingú River region, South America. (After Steinen.)

Differences of social class hardly exist among these people. Elders tend to be respected by their juniors (in contrast to our own society) and there is a headman or chief in each community, but his authority is slight. The most respected – and feared – person is the medicine man or sorcerer who is believed to command magic powers and to be able to transform himself into a man-eating jaguar.

THE TIKOPIA

Tikopia is a small volcanic island on the eastern edge of the Solomons group in Polynesia. It is barely four square miles in area and is inhabited by about twelve hundred natives. These people are finely built, tall and medium brown in colour. The men let their hair grow into a long bushy mane; the women wear theirs close cropped. These people are agriculturists and fishermen. Their crops include coconuts, yams, taro, breadfruit, sago, bananas, pawpaws, manioc and sugar cane. Their traditional tools were adzes with blades made from clam shells, bamboo knives and simple digging sticks, but nowadays they have European steel tools which they obtain by simple trading. For fishing they use thorn hooks, a multiple pronged spear, and nets of sinnit. Flying fish are sometimes caught from canoes with a kind of gaff or butterfly net. Much of the food is cooked – some quite elaborately – by putting it on hot stones in a shallow pit and covering it with layers of leaves. When not eating they often chew betel nuts which stain lips and mouth a brilliant red.

Their simple clothing is mostly made from bark cloth. Their rectangular houses have low-pitched gabled roofs thatched with sago palm; these have several doors, each so low that entry can only be made by crawling on hands and knees. The only light filters in between the thatch; the only furnishing consists of a few mats of plaited coconut spread out on the floor beneath which the dead ancestors of the family are buried.

Villages contain up to thirty of these dwellings and are surrounded by orchards, gardens and plantations. There is hereditary ownership of these plots and the extent of individual wealth (which is based on them) varies more than among the Witotoan.

Class differences are found. The most important social unit is a family or kinship group called a *paito* or 'houses'. These family lines are of three sorts – noble, high commoner and low commoner. These *paito* have chiefs at their head who are entitled to respect and to certain privileges such as the right to settle quarrels, to receive gifts and, especially, to play an important role in rituals dedicated to the worship of their gods. Their privileges are, as usual, balanced by obligations such as the duty to care for their kinfolk and to ensure the welfare of their *paito*. As is common among the peoples of Oceania, families of Tikopia trace their descent through many generations.

THE TUNGUS

A quite different sort of food production is found among the Tungus who live in the far north-east of Siberia. This area has one of the harshest climates in the world. Snow lies almost continuously all the year round and brief thaws of the drifts and rivers last for only a few weeks in high summer. The density of population here is sometimes as low as one person for every hundred and fifty square miles. All the Tungus of this region hunt bears, elk, wild reindeer and small animals. They all fish in the rivers whenever the ice melts.

But they are also food producers because they are one of the groups of people who have tamed reindeer and keep them in domestic herds, just as the Lapps do on a much larger scale. Strangely, they do not greatly use them for meat. The women milk them and this provides one of their most important foods, but they make neither butter nor cheese.

The men use the reindeer to ride on and also as pack animals, provided the load is no more than about ten stone. For this purpose they usually saw off the antlers to save the rider from being knocked off whenever the animal turns its head round. Reindeer make good draught animals and can travel fifty miles a day even when harnessed to a light sledge. Another use for them is as decoys for the wild reindeer, which are the chief source of meat for the Tungus of this area. Sometimes the hunters tie leather thongs round the antlers of a tame reindeer and drive it out towards a wild herd. A wild stag will then attack it and its antlers become entangled among the thongs so that the hunters can come up and shoot it with bow and arrows.

The mosses, lichens and plant stalks which are the reindeer's food are often in short supply or buried under hard snow. So the herds have to be kept continually moving and seldom stay more than a few hours in one place.

For a short time in the summer Tungus families may gather in groups of a few hundred people. For the rest of the year they are usually widely scattered in small family parties. They have no great differences in wealth and there are no hereditary chiefs. Decisions about the daily life of the people are made by agreement between the older and most respected members of the clans.

In spite of the great differences between the ways in which *Simple Food Producers* live they are alike in many respects:

(*a*) Populations are never dense and villages seldom exceed a few hundred people.

(*b*) In all these groups hunting, fishing and collecting food remains extremely important, in addition to whatever cultivation of plants or domestication of animals may be practised.

(*c*) The land and most sources of food supply are shared in common by the villagers although a few private gardens, pools, trees or animals may exist.

(d) Apart from a few of the pastoral groups, food producers usually stay much longer in one place than food gatherers.

(e) This means that their houses are often more elaborate and remain in one place for several years.

(f) There is more surplus food available, so barter with neighbouring tribes is more developed, though rarely extensive.

(g) Because food is more plentiful there is also more leisure time in which people can make musical instruments, jewelry, ornaments, fancy woven cloth or decorated pottery and other objects that are not essential to bare survival.

(h) Hence more persons become specialists in some art or craft.

(i) Occasional feuds and forays take place between rival clans or tribes but true war hardly occurs. Sometimes these fighting expeditions are seasonal and take place after the harvest has been gathered.

(j) Slight differences in personal wealth may be found but these are never extreme and are usually limited to non-essential objects such as house furniture or ornaments.

(k) There are no great differences in rank. Village headmen or tribal chiefs are merely well respected or popular persons. They have no great wealth and their power is based on personality and prestige, not sanctioned by high rank. At the other extreme there is no great class of serfs or slaves, though lazy individuals will no doubt tend to own less than their more energetic neighbours.

In contrast to the Witoto, Tungus or Tikopia, who enjoy an economy only a little above subsistence level, there are many peoples who can be described as *Advanced Food Producers*.

As an example of these we can look at the Yoruba of West Africa. They number about 10,000,000 people and inhabit a large part of Nigeria, a hot, wet country with large savanna or grassland clearings in between patches of woodland and forest.

The Yoruba are farmers who produce many crops. These include bananas, maize, gourds, millet, ground nuts, cassava, beans and a little rice. But yams are the most important of all. Several kinds are grown and they can be harvested throughout the year. They also keep a few goats, cattle and chickens, but not enough to supply much meat. In some parts of the country wild game – chiefly the many sorts of antelope – is plentiful, and here the animals are pursued by men specializing as hunters.

Wild plants are much used, especially the oil palm which provides a most important ingredient in cooking and is also used for lighting. From another wild plant, the raffia palm, wine is made by cutting into the bark and collecting the sap which is then fermented.

The constant hard work of these industrious Yoruba farmers results in heavy crops and often in a large surplus of food. Barter of a simple kind exists but real trade on an extensive scale is much more important. Many areas, often whole villages, specialize in some way either by making salt, in sea or river fishing, in hunting, mixed farming, the production of palm oil and much else.

Many special crafts are carried on that have no direct connection with food production. There are potters, metal workers, weavers, wood carvers, boat builders and ivory workers. Women are important as independent traders. They form guilds of craft-workers and may, in their own right, become wealthier than their husbands. In many towns women advise the *oba* – the district chief – and his council on affairs affecting their sex.

As a result of this advanced and complicated economy the picture presented by societies which are *Advanced Food Producers* is very different from that of the Simple Food Gatherers or Producers and may be summed up as follows:

(*a*) Populations are dense, with large villages and towns, some of which contain many thousands of inhabitants, such as Timbuctoo, Ibadan and Benin.

(*b*) Great inequality of wealth is found: some men or families become extremely rich, others are reduced to poverty. In Cochin, in southern India, 90 per cent of the land is still owned by less than 5 per cent of the people.

(*c*) Differences in rank accompany this: great chieftains or noblemen arise and all intermediate social levels may be found down to slave populations at the bottom of the scale. These positions are often hereditary.

(*d*) Great specialization is found among craftsmen, especially among the men, although women also have their specialities, such as trading in the markets.

(*e*) This leads to the development of trade across widespread areas of country, large markets and the use of real money as a medium of exchange, as well as complicated credit systems.

(*f*) A richly varied social and political life develops with an elaborate system of law to keep the country working smoothly. Taxes and tribute from the people are raised in many ways, and are usually controlled by the central government which often contains people who can read and write.

(*g*) The surplus of wealth enables full-scale wars to be carried on, sometimes with men who do little else but serve as soldiers. (At one time the kings of Yoruba used to keep a large army of cavalry which gave them a great advantage over some of their neighbours.)

(*h*) Finally we can say that, in contrast to the more primitive types of basic economy which are very conservative and slow to change, these *Advanced Food Producing* states often tend to change rapidly.

Not all these characteristics are invariably found in these societies. For example, there may be no slaves. The development of traits varies, too, from one culture to another but, in general, such populations exhibit many or most of the features listed here.

In this sketch of some of the ways by which primitive peoples get their food, a few items have been briefly listed. Little more than a collection of isolated culture traits has been set down. It is important to stress, however, that here again culture complexes and elaborately integrated systems are found. One example must suffice. Eskimo whaling was dismissed above in a single word: in fact much could be said about it.

The Alaskan Whale Cult is an elaborate complex of technological, economic, socio-political and magico-religious elements. The technical aspect involves a complicated apparatus of boats, paddles, harpoons, floats, lines and clothing, together with skills

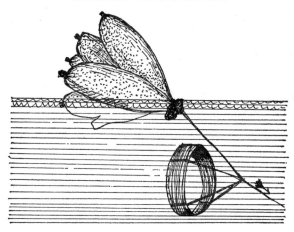

32 Inflated seal skins and drag. To exhaust a harpooned whale and to reveal its position. (After Boas.)

to locate, track, attack, kill and land the animal, with its subsequent disposal (Fig. 32). All this is woven into an intricate web of beliefs and customs, of which the following items are only a small part:

(1) Leadership in a whale hunt is integrated with social leadership.

(2) Distribution of the parts of the whale follows strict rules which give special rights to the boat owner, harpooner and others.

(3) Initiation into the Whale Cult is only to be had after a long period of arduous instruction.

(4) Magical amulets and good luck tokens are used.

(5) Privately owned whaling songs are sung.

(6) Special ceremonials and taboos are associated with the whaling season: the whalers are ritually unclean and must sleep in the open and eat no raw meat; the people who remain in the village must refrain from sleep and food whilst the hunt is on.

(7) All the hunting gear must be clean and repaired before the whaling season begins, so as not to offend the whale.

(8) The landed whale is given a symbolic drink by the whaler's wife.

(9) When the animal is cut up, special rituals are performed so that the whale's spirit may return to the sea unangered.

(10) The ritual period after killing a whale is the same as that following a human death.

Much more could be added, but this is enough to show how even such a basic and direct activity as putting meals into mouths is interwoven with many of the most fundamental postulates and attitudes of the culture. This is another example of the organization of culture. The various complexes which surround the food quest serve psychologically to allay the ever-present fear that starvation may lurk ahead. They also reinforce, symbolically and in action, the solidarity and interdependence of the people who make up a society.

The peoples discussed in this chapter may be described, by our earlier criteria and to different degrees, as 'primitive' – always bearing in mind the ultimate relativity of the term. But people in the advanced civilizations also need to eat, and this normally entails a much more complicated process of acquiring and distributing food than any we have met so far. The chief difference is that, in the advanced societies such as England, Germany and many others, only a very small percentage of the population are farmers or gardeners producing significant quantities of food. The overwhelming majority of people regularly eat food but rarely produce it. They are the urbanized factory workers, the shop-keepers, bank clerks, civil servants, insurance brokers, truck drivers, policemen and school teachers who may grow a few backyard cabbages and tomatoes but seldom enough to give them more than half a dozen meals in a year. Most people in large cities do not even do this.

There are, of course, countries such as Canada where grain, roots, fruit, meat and dairy production is at such a high level that the population could easily be fed from national resources, despite the existence of a few large urban areas. But in small, densely populated countries like England or Belgium, agricultural land is far too scarce to grow enough food for all the inhabitants.

It follows, therefore, that these nations must import most of what they eat. This can only be done through the complicated mechanism of international trade, with its elaborate systems of credits, payment, shipping, refrigeration, canning, and distribution by rail, road or retailer. The whole process must then be geared into the intricacies of the total social and cultural system of many different nations. Space does not permit any aspect of these vast manoeuvres to be discussed here, but it is important to remember that they exist and that they are proper subjects for anthropological study.

6 SOCIETY (I)

People living together

Social structure, the family, monogamy, polygyny, polyandry, kinship terms, incest, exogamy, sim-pua, preferential marriage, endogamy, castes, lineage, affinal marriage, progeny-price, residence after marriage, divorce, descent, clan, phratry, totemism, extended families.

All over the world, wherever they are found at all, people live in groups. These groups may be very large, as in the teeming millions of great cities like Tokyo, London and Calcutta; they may be small, as in the villages of rural England, of the Kelabits of Borneo and the Tikopia of Polynesia; or they may be tiny, as in the almost isolated families of some Eskimo and Chukchi. But whether populations are large or small they always have this feature that people live in company with one another, not alone.

We call such a group of people a *society* and we may guess that from the earliest days of his evolution man has always lived in this way. He is not a solitary animal. But the essence of society, as anthropologists use the word, is not the mere living together in herds. It is the fact that these groups have what is called *social structure*, which means that they are divided into units such as families, tribes or nations that have recognizable forms and which are interrelated in more or less clearly defined ways. In some of these social groupings membership is voluntary, in others there is no option. A man cannot choose to be born into a family or clan but he may be free to marry into one of his choice, to select his tennis club or, in West Africa, to apply for entry into the *Nanamei Akpee* 'mutual help' society. In general, people have much more freedom of choice in the higher civilizations than among primitive cultures where the social structure is often rigidly fixed on a basis of kinship, hereditary class or place of residence. But whether there is much or little freedom of choice the key to understanding is to see it as a functioning whole; to realize that patterns of kinship and marriage, of magic, religion and taboos, or divisions of class and clan always hang together in a coherent system which

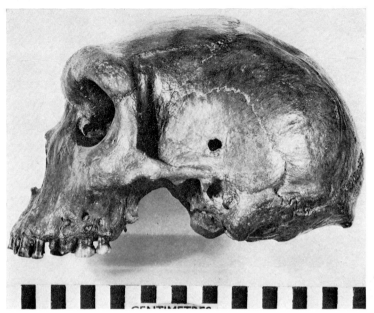

I The skull from Broken Hill, Rhodesia. This is a late and specialized Neandertaloid type, dating from c. 40,000 B.C. British Museum.

II This young Dane is wearing an exact copy of the pullover, corded mini-skirt, large bronze buckle and bracelets which had been preserved on the body of a Bronze Age girl found at Egtved, Denmark. *Photo: The Danish National Museum.*

III Malay fishermen at Penang draw a catch on to the sands. As elsewhere, this is men's work. *Photo: Radio Times.*

IV An Eskimo mother with her children outside
her summer tent. *Photo: Radio Times.*

v Outside her grass roofed hut a Bushman mother pours her son a drink from a skin "bottle". His tin dish is of European origin. *Photo: Radio Times.*

vi Two Bushman youths. They are sucking up water through a long reed and spitting it into ostrich shell "bottles" for future use. *Photo: Radio Times.*

VII In Old Dehli, India, a man of the low caste of potters sits outside his shack. *Photo: Radio Times.*

VIII Australian aborigines wearing the extensive body painting that accompanies many of their ceremonies. Compare this with Plate XVI. *Photo: Radio Times.*

x A Haitian voodoo dancer is going into ecstasia or trance as he joins in a wild dance with the white-shirted priest. *Photo: Radio Times.*

IX A Tongan fisherman using a flare to attract fish by night. He catches them with a pronged spear. *Photo: Radio Times.*

XI An elder of the village of Mudichur, Madras, at his devotions. He has washed, painted the caste-marks on his forehead and arms, and now prays to Vishnu for peace. *Photo: Radio Times.*

XII In 1950, Seretse Khama, Chief of the Bamangwato married an English woman. Here a group of his subjects are discussing the legal aspects of the event. They have assembled in the "Kgotla", the meeting place for formal tribal gatherings. *Photo: Radio Times.*

XIII A Mochica pot from precolumbian Peru. Many of these water jugs take the form of a naturalistic portrayal of people or animals. This one shows a face deformed by the disease *uta*. British Museum.

XIV A wooden mask from Nigeria, Ohafia, Ibo tribe. It represents a one-eyed man who cannot find his mouth to use his chewing stick to clean his teeth. It is used in a mime associated with the New Yam Festival. Lagos, Nigerian Museum. *Photo: K. C. Murray.*

xv Nigeria. Native dancers and musicians performing a rain-making ceremony. Kadura. *Photo: Radio Times.*

xvi Evonne Goolagong, an aborigine, who is one of the most promising of the younger Australian tennis players. *Photo: The Age, Melbourne.*

keeps the total order integrated and smoothly working. Indeed, the integration is so close that the different parts of it may be said to determine each other's pattern. Another result of this cohesion is that, for any society, the whole is always greater than the sum of its parts.

Some confusion is likely to occur because the word 'society' is often used in two quite distinct senses – as can be seen from the preceding paragraph. In its general sociological sense it is usually applied to the largest embracing social group, and this is nearly always coterminous, both on the ground and as regards membership, with the widest politically organized unit: village, clan or nation. The second use applies it to small associations, frequently voluntary, within the larger group and which are often equivalent to the various units which we cover by such terms as club, fraternity, lodge, college, guild or sodality. It is essential to recognize which of these two meanings is being used.

We shall now take a brief look at some of the more important features which determine social structure.

The most fundamental of all social groups is the *family*, a group which serves several basic functions. Of these we may mention four. (1) It allots different roles to the males and females of whom it is composed, the main purpose of this being (2) to provide for the care and rearing of children; (3) it forms a starting point for the transmission of culture from one generation to the next; and (4) it gives social approval to sex relations between husbands and wives.

Two types of family organization are found: conjugal and consanguine.

The centre of a *conjugal family* is a man and his wife (who may be cousins but are often unrelated by blood) together with their children and a surrounding fringe of relatives who serve to connect them with other similar families.

A family of this kind takes several years to develop into a smoothly running unit. Its nucleus always remains small and as the children mature they play a very important part in it. When they leave to marry and form families of their own the parental group is much weakened and disrupted. Because conjugal families end when the original partners die it may happen that elderly or young dependents are left uncared for, lands and property may be switched to other controlling groups or split between several

F

descendants. Eskimo, Bushman and English families are organized on the conjugal pattern.

A different type of organization is seen in *consanguine families*. Here the nucleus is a group of kindred whose relationship, biological or by adoption, can be shown genealogically in a family 'tree' of descent. In such a family when children grow up and want to marry they do not hive off from the nucleus and set up splinter families of their own. They bring their partners into the already existing consanguine family. No time is lost in learning mutual adjustments because brothers, cousins, aunts, uncles and grandchildren have lived all their lives together. These families persist for generations, they can extend to become far bigger units than the small conjugal nucleus, they are better adapted for supporting their aged and their young, as well as for embarking on large co-operative enterprises. When occasional individuals leave the consanguine nucleus there is little disruption or weakening of the social structure within it. Persons who marry into a family of this type are called *affinal* kin.

It is quite common, in European or North American society, for people not to marry. Moreover, they find no great difficulty from remaining single. If a bachelor cannot cook he devises a simple breakfast of instant coffee, cornflakes, toast and marmalade; for lunch he goes out to a restaurant or his factory canteen; and in the evening returns home to a supper that is prepared for him by a neighbour or daily help who cooks the meal in return for an appropriate wage. The spinster may be a professional woman or a business executive. If she cannot cope with filling domestic boilers, digging the garden and other housework, she hires a charwoman, a gardener or a daily maid to run her house. Alternatively she lives in a service flat where everything is done for her. Neither of these persons need be inconvenienced by their lack of a mate.

No such easy survival is open to an unmarried person in a primitive tribe. For an Eskimo woman to survive she needs a husband who can go off, perhaps for days at a time, hunting caribou or seals. For an Eskimo man a wife is essential to look after the chores of the igloo, to prepare skins, clothing, harness, blubber, food, and to care for the children. In almost all simple societies, with basic economies which yield little surplus, life is impossible or intolerable without a marriage partner. The division of work between males and females is often so marked that the only practicable solution is for a man and woman to live and work together as a team.

In almost all countries and tribes the number of adult men is approximately equal to the number of women. As a result, by far the commonest form of marriage is between one man and one woman. This is called *monogamy*. It is the form with which we are familiar in the modern Western societies because it is our only legal one. To go through a ceremony of marriage with a second man or woman whilst any previous marriage still continues is to commit the crime of bigamy.

Though monogamy is certain to be the best known type of marriage to us, if we are Europeans or Americans, it is not the only form. Most societies throughout the world approve of *polygamy*, in which a person has more than one legal spouse at the same time. It can take the form of either *polygyny* or *polyandry*. Polygyny means that a man is married to more than one wife; polyandry, that a woman has more than one husband.

Almost all tribal societies and many advanced ones favour polygyny as a desirable pattern of marriage even though few of their members achieve it. The Islamic or Moslem countries, for example, permit a man to have up to four wives. But as we have already said, in most populations (even when they approve of polygyny) the rule is still monogamy because of the nearly equal numbers of the sexes. Under these circumstances one man can have two wives only by denying some other man the chance of finding one.

There are a few exceptions where females do outnumber males. Among the Eskimo, hunting is so dangerous that a number of men get killed, thus leaving a small surplus of women, but this only permits about one man in twenty to take a second wife. He is usually some outstanding hunter. Men of Tikopia, a Polynesian island, often lost their lives at sea: the resulting excess of women allowed a few of the chiefs to take several wives. To the Yakö of Nigeria polygyny was possible because they bought young girls from foreign tribes and to the Rangi of Tanzania because many young men emigrated to work for white employers.

In practice polygyny is not only limited by the negligible surplus of women. It is also restricted by the inability of the average man to support more than one wife and family. Only an exceptionally skilful Eskimo hunter can cope with the demands made by a double marriage: it may carry prestige but is likely to be intolerable. So wherever a simple food-gathering economy is found polygyny, though permitted, is rare in practice. In advanced food-producing societies, in the West African Yoruba for example, headmen and upper ranks often support several wives whilst the great chiefs or kings may have hundreds but the mass of the population still have only one. The need to provide bride-price is a further restriction on polygyny in many societies. In the Hehe tribe of Tanzania of 3,028 married men, 62 per cent had one wife, 26 per cent had two wives and only 1 per cent had more than four. On the other hand, apart from any prestige that may attach to a man who has several wives, in some societies polygyny gives solid and practical advantages. It can offer a chance to strengthen economic interests and plural wives serve to build up a large body of kinsmen. If the wives are well chosen, influential links may be forged in the political, territorial or religious spheres of social activity. It may also be valued for the assurance it is likely to provide for the continuation of the male or female line, or for its part in ancestor worship.

Polygyny need not be degrading to the women though sometimes it is felt to be so even in societies where it is common. There is no general rule about this. Since it can be practised by only the richest or most skilful men it often has high status value. So much so that a solitary wife may urge her husband to take a second wife who will be a companion to her when he is away from home and who will work beside her in the house and fields. This second wife is almost always approved, if not actually chosen, by the first. Sometimes she will be her own younger sister, in which case we speak of *sororal polygyny*. A common pattern, as seen among the Lango of East Africa and the Tanala of Madagascar, is for each wife to have a separate house, granary and garden but to combine with the others in doing the necessary work, especially out of doors. Relations between co-wives are not always halcyon, however: many cases of jealousy and quarrelling have been recorded from polygynous groups and the first wife may resent the intrusion of a second, perhaps younger and more attractive one. The themes of many Chinese novels and folk literature testify to this. Ashanti co-wives call each other *kora*, i.e. 'jealous one'. In many African societies a first wife, especially of a chief or headman, greatly outranks any subsequent wives and this may more than off-set any disadvantages. Though not as rare as formerly believed, polyandry is much less common than polygyny. Why this is so is uncertain. It may be related to innate tendencies toward male dominance or it may be, in general, a less efficient system in its sociological functioning. Today Tibet is the largest and most flourishing polyandrous community, but it has also been reported from the Marquesans of Polynesia, the Shoshone of Idaho, the Palawan of the Philippines, the Kota of southern India and various other groups. The Toda, a tribe of buffalo dairy farmers in southern India, have long been a classic example.

Different forms of polyandry occur. The commonest is *fraternal*, where one or more wives are shared by a group of brothers. Various explanations of the custom have been suggested. Female infanticide (the killing of girl babies) is said to account for it with the Toda but the infanticide could as well be a result of polyandry as its cause. It is extensively practised, together with monogamy and polygyny, by the Pahari Hindus from Kashmir to Nepal. Among them property is owned by patrilineal, patrilocal extended families, and polyandry may serve in part to keep land and property within the group, at the same time reducing the number of heirs who will inherit it. The suggestion has been made that in some groups polyandry is favoured where women have valuable dowries and property rights. This does not apply to the Pahari. Amity within the fraternal group seems to be increased by the custom, but jealousies do occur. Socially, polyandry can be seen as a group transaction in which a family collectively acquires the economic, sexual and reproductive services of a woman. The fraternal unity itself is, in Jaunsar Bawar, expressed in economic, ritual and social relations. Pahari polyandry, as in many other parts of India, derives its sanctions from religious tradition, notably from the ancient *Mahabharata* epic which tells of the exploits of the five Pandara brothers and their common wife Draupadi.

Pahari groups show striking differences in the sex ratio: some have more men than women, others more women than men. In the former, polyandry is common; in the latter, polygyny. But this strong correlation is quite absent in other groups.

Wherever polyandry is found the biological father of any children must always be uncertain. The Toda get round this difficulty by paying no attention to biology; for them paternity is a social, not a physiological, fact. One of the husbands performs a ceremony which attaches the child to his own clan and safeguards its interests. The situation is resolved by other tribes in various ways.

Earlier anthropologists used to believe that the beginnings of primitive marriage were to be found in *promiscuity*: a condition in which any men of the tribe mated at random with any women, all constantly changing partners and never settling to permanent relationships. No society has ever been found in which this behaviour can be traced. It seems a highly improbable pattern because its lack of stability would be too prejudicial for the survival of their babies (Fig. 33).

Marriage by capture seems hardly to occur in any society. Token struggles between the bride and bridegroom before the wedding ceremony have been interpreted as survivals of early marriage by capture. It is more likely that they merely symbolize interlineage hostility and the sense of loss or resentment felt by the bride's family.

Group marriage is defined as a state in which a number of men are married to a number of women and there is complete interchange within the group. At one time its occurrence seems to have been surmised by anthropologists who failed to understand the kinship terminology of primitive tribes.

Two sorts of terms may be used to describe kinship relationships. *Descriptive* terms refer to one type of relationship only, such as our 'mother', 'father', 'sister'. *Classificatory* terms refer to more than one type. For example, 'grandfather' can mean either father's father or mother's father, 'aunt' can mean father's or mother's sister, while 'cousin' can be father's brother's child (male or female), father's sister's child or the equivalents on the maternal side. The terms used by primitive peoples vary but tend to be more classificatory than ours. This partly reflects the larger role played by extended kinship groups in such societies, compared with our narrow conjugal families.

In Hawaii the classificatory system is virtually absolute. Apart from a gender change to indicate the sex of the relative (as in French *cousin–cousine* or Italian *figlio–figlia*) only a classification in terms of generation is used. So all relatives of one's own generation are called brother or sister, all of the previous genera-

33 Baby in a hanging chair. Cubeo tribe, north-west Amazonia. (After Koch-Grünberg.)

tions are 'parent' or 'grandparent', whilst those of succeeding generations are all 'child' or 'grandchild'. It is systems of this sort that are likely to suggest group marriage, because several men and women will be called by the same terms as are used for the real biological parents.

We have only one word for all cousins but many peoples distinguish between *parallel* and *cross* cousins. Parallel cousins are so called because the parents through whom they are related are of the same sex; cross cousins are related through parents of opposite sex. Figure 34 shows the difference.

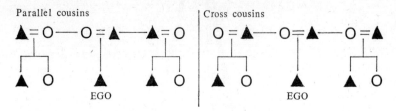

Parallel cousins | Cross cousins

EGO   EGO

34 This shows the difference between parallel and cross cousins.

Tribes which distinguish between the two types of cousins rarely reckon cross cousins as belonging to the same kindred group. To marry a parallel cousin may count as incest, almost certainly so if the partners are of the same clan. To marry a cross cousin (who is genetically just as close) is often the most desirable marriage.

Unlike the Hawaiian system, Eskimo terms distinguish siblings from cousins. But, like us, they lump together parallel and cross cousins. The Sudanese terminology contrasts strongly with the Hawaiian type in being an almost entirely descriptive system so that different terms are applied to each sort of cousin, aunt, uncle, nephew, niece, sibling, etc. Other systems exist but the variations are never mere linguistic oddities in a cultural vacuum. They always reflect the social structure in such matters as the different emphasis which each society places on patrilineal or matrilineal descent and inheritance.

A convenient classification can be based on the terms used to describe the parents, uncles and aunts. Figure 35 shows four such systems.

SYSTEM	SEPARATE DESCRIPTIVE TERMS FOR		SIMILAR CLASSIFICATORY TERMS FOR	
	Males	*Females*	*Males*	*Females*
A	Father	Mother		
	Father's brother	Mother's sister		
	Mother's brother	Father's sister		
B	Father	Mother	Father's brother	Mother's sister
			Mother's brother	Father's sister
C			Father	Mother
			Father's brother	Mother's sister
			Mother's brother	Father's sister
D	Mother's brother	Father's sister	Father	Mother
			Father's brother	Mother's sister

35 One method of classifying societies according to their kinship
terminology.

In areas where clans are uncommon, that is where the family
does not compete with unilateral groups, either A or B predomi-
nates. Where clans are the rule, as in the United States east of the
Missouri, the south-west, and northern British Columbia, type D
is the commonest system. Type C is typical of many Polynesians.
The Kwakiutl have no strict clans, since they permit marriage
with a brother's daughter, and their terminology is of type B. But
the northern Kwakiutl (Haisla), who do have clans, use the D
system. The clanless Tewa of New Mexico use descriptive terms,
but the one Tewa group settled among the Hopi pueblo dwellers

shares the Hopi clan organization and uses the classificatory D system.

Some primitive kinship systems use one term when speaking *to* a relative but another term when speaking *of* him. Thus, a native of Tikopia addresses his father as 'Pa' but refers to him as 'Tamana'.

Some of these ways of classifying relatives may appear unnecessarily complicated. For instance, the Comanche of the American Plains have thirty-six kinship categories. One result of this complexity is that it enables a person to know on whom he may call for help in such tasks as house-building, digging his garden or collecting progeny price when he wants to marry. When he calls his father's brothers 'father' it is a way of emphasizing that their social relationship to him is almost as close as his real father. In turn, he treats them with the respect due from a son. In many societies there is a very special relationship between a man and his mother's brother. This normally has profound social consequences.

As well as positive kinship obligations, there are universal negative rules prohibiting sexual relations between real or fictional relatives. These are the rules of the *incest* taboo. In England, a man cannot marry his mother, sister or daughter. Until 1907 he could not even marry his deceased wife's sister. But there is no objection to a marriage between cousins. Most primitives extend the incest taboo to include more remote kinsfolk than we do – sometimes a whole clan, regardless of biological relationship. Details vary but the interesting fact is the general similarity of incest rules in hundreds of different societies all over the world. People cannot, of course, marry within a group which, to them, is covered by an incest taboo. They have to marry outside it and this form of marriage is called *exogamy*. The conjugal family is always exogamous, lineages and clans usually so. One result of exogamy is to ally two separate social units and strengthen each in its economic, social and political ramifications. It binds small social groups by ties of affinal kinship, giving a wider integration to society.

The origin of the incest taboo is puzzling. It used to be said that it expressed an instinctive biological horror or that it was a device to prevent deterioration of the stock by inbreeding. Neither explanation can be true. We have no horror about marrying a first cousin, who is genetically quite close to us, whereas a Karadjeri Australian would recoil from marrying someone only tenuously related to him by our standards. Nor does inbreeding necessarily lead to loss of vigour if the original stock is sound. It is difficult to find a better explanation for the prohibition than that suggested by Malinowski. He noted the fact that, within the family, sexual association is permitted between the spouses. He also noted the powerful emotional disturbance which can be generated by sexual drives and the disrupting influence they can have when given unrestricted play amongst those nearest at hand, between father and daughter or mother and son, for instance. Therefore, to preserve the integrity of the close kin group, sexual rivalry must be eliminated. Hence the universality of incest prohibitions and the often severe penalties inflicted on people who transgress them. For example, the Ashanti and many Australian tribes punish incest with death.

Whilst discussing incest, we may mention a Chinese custom which was common on the Yangtze delta and in South China, until recent reform of the marriage laws. *T'ung-yang-hsi* or sim-pua are girls who are adopted into a family as daughters so that when they grow up they can become daughters-in-law by marrying a son. This form of wedding (*hsiao-hun*) is socially despised but cheap. Its alternative (*ta-hun*), in which the bride is already a young adult, is a much more highly esteemed ceremony but is expensive. It may cost the bridegroom's family from six months' to more than a year's gross income. Sim-pua are almost always badly treated but, because they have lived from infancy in the family where they are eventually wives, hsiao-hun marriages are less full of generational tensions than ta-hun, in which the new bride comes unadjusted to her mother-in-law and may seek to seduce her husband away from his filial duty. Sim-pua are, in effect, first sisters then wives to the same person. This gives rise to some emotional ambivalence as far as sexual relations are concerned. As a way of circumventing incest prohibitions it is a custom that fits completely into one of the few societies in which parents have full authority over their adult offspring.

To avoid confusion, a clear distinction should be made between incest rules, which apply to sexual relations, and exogamy, which applies to marriage between socially defined persons irrespective of genealogical relationship. Both customs serve to maintain the existing kinship structure and to avoid disrupting the established system.

Marriage is such a basic and important element in the social structure that most societies do not leave it to the caprice of individual choice. As well as the incest taboos, they have rules defining whom a person ought to, or must, marry. These are the rules of *preferential marriage*. Their form and function varies from one society to another but a few examples will illustrate their significance.

The converse of exogamy is *endogamy*, which means that a person has to marry within a prescribed social group of which he or she is a member. From what has been said about incest it will be clear that endogamy within a family or clan is rare. The best known example of endogamy is the caste system of India.

Castes, of which there are about a couple of thousand, are rigidly fixed groups in which membership is hereditary and theoretically inescapable. They are also, in theory, occupational units (Plate VII). Originally they evolved from a system of ideas claiming religious sanction and this is still an important feature of the Hindu outlook. Marriage within one's own caste was almost universal throughout the system though, as always in social groupings, the rules are occasionally bent to meet special circumstances. Castes are graded in a sweep of social status from the highest Brahman or Rajput units down to the untouchables and those, such as leather workers, whose mere approach causes ritual atmospheric pollution of members of the higher grades. The system secures the powerful and favoured position of the dominant castes who have much to lose by its abolition. A modification of the normal caste marriage pattern is *hypergamy*, in which a girl marries a man in a higher sub-caste or of higher status in her own caste. This is practised in Cochin and elsewhere. It puts a premium on eligible men, since a high caste girl may find it difficult to obtain a husband of even higher status. Castes also function as legal units because they can expel members who offend against their codes of behaviour, and today many of them are becoming important as political pressure groups, whose cohesion and strength are rooted in the traditional solidarity of their members. Once again, it should be noted that, as in innumerable other social groups, actual behaviour of castes and individuals is often far removed from the ideal pattern or what allegedly happens. An example of this is the occupation of Brahmans. By definition these are priestly castes and the top-ranking members of the hierarchy.

But they still retain Brahman status although they often perform no religious duties and may be employed as scribes, farmers, soldiers, shepherds or cooks.

Less well developed caste systems are found in Africa and elsewhere. The Ruanda are divided into a ruling pastoral nobility, the Tussi, a group of horticulturists, the Hutu, and a lowly hunting caste, the Twa. Endogamy is practised, with something less than complete rigidity, by each division. The Ankole kingdom of Uganda has a complicated class structure, much of which is filled by the relationships of a ruling pastoral group, the Bahima, with a repressed caste of agriculturists, the Bairu. Group endogamy is reinforced by a prohibition on the Bairu ownership of cattle – which are necessary to valid Bahima marriages.

The terms exogamy and endogamy should strictly apply only when each custom is obligatory, not when it is optional. In practice this usage is not always observed, and by extension the term *religious endogamy* is loosely used to cover the tendency for orthodox Catholics to marry within their own faith. Nazism, for bogus reasons of racism, enforced endogamy on German Jews during the Hitler régime. Until recently the European nobility tended to marry amongst themselves, thus practising weak *class endogamy*. All these forms of marriage function to integrate and stabilize social groups which, for various reasons, want to retain their identity.

In many primitive societies the most important unit in the social structure is the *lineage*, an extended unilateral kinship group descended from a known ancestor. Lineages are almost invariably exogamous and interlineage marriage is a powerful device for increasing their social, political and economic status. An exception is found among certain Arab communities where a man has a legal right to marry his father's brother's daughter – his parallel cousin. In most societies, except a few like our own, this would be an incestuous relationship. Its occurrence among the Arabs appears to reflect the facts that a man inherits land solely from his own lineage; military power is focused in each separate unit; and political union of lineages is uncommon and unstable. Hence little is gained and much lost by marrying away from one's kinsmen. For modern city Arabs these considerations hardly apply, so parallel cousin marriage is no longer observed by them.

Far more common than this Arab oddity is cross-cousin

marriage. This is the preferred or obligatory marriage in a great number of tribes, including most Australians and many Melanesians and Africans. It is also found in Californian Indians and other American groups. It may be *symmetrical*, in which the spouse can be related through either the father or the mother; or it may be *asymmetrical*, either patrilineal as among the Haida Indians and the Trobriand Islanders or matrilineal as with the Sirionó of Eastern Bolivia. The reason for the particular variety in which cross-cousin marriage occurs in a tribe is usually determined by its social structure and specific kinship organization. Why it should be practised at all is more open to argument. In tribes with a clan system it is easy to see that parallel cousins may belong to the same clan; but cross cousins never do and therefore do not count as relatives. Hence, marriage of cross cousins is permissible and is a way of stabilizing social relations between kinship groups by recurrent marital linkage.

Another type of marriage – sometimes optional, sometimes obligatory – is *affinal* or *continuation* marriage. These unions, between persons who are already 'in-laws', serve to continue the relationship between two kin groups after one of the partners has died.

When a man dies, it becomes the right or duty of one of his brothers to marry the widow. This is known as the *levirate* (Latin *levir*, brother-in-law). Conversely, on the death of a woman her sister has the right or duty to marry the widower. This is the *sororate*. (The word is also used in other senses.) The two customs commonly go hand in hand and are extremely widespread. Several variations occur but they all have similar functions. In most societies marriage is far more than a bond between husband and wife. It unites two kinship groups and this alliance is strengthened by the levirate, which ensures that neither the wife nor the children of the original husband are lost to his kin group. The Nuer of the Sudan, and many other peoples, extend this principle: any later children born to the widow are legally the offspring of her dead husband. This is often associated with ancestor worship and the need for a man to have descendants who will act for him in the future. Indeed, so important is this that, with the Nuer, if even an unmarried man dies without having left sons, it is the duty of one of his kinsmen to marry on his behalf and rear sons in the name of the dead man. This practice is known as *ghost marriage*.

The levirate also ensures that the claims of the widow's kin upon her husband's family are maintained through the brother-in-law who becomes the new husband. And, apart from the children's position, the widow is not left unsupported in societies where women have difficulty in surviving without male help. The sororate guarantees that a man who has handed over progeny-price to another kin group shall retain the privileges which became due to him, even if his wife dies.

In some societies similar functions are served by affinal marriages between uncles and nieces-in-law, aunts and nephews-in-law, or other relatives.

Brother-sister marriage is known from Hawaii, some Congo tribes, ancient Egypt and the Incas of Peru. It was always a prerogative of the ruling group and functioned to keep the inheritance of wealth or titles within the dynasty, usually under the guise of maintaining unsullied the divine kingship to which these groups laid claim. *Father-daughter marriage*, which also occurred in ancient Egypt, served the same purpose.

We have just referred to *progeny-price* or, as it is often called, *bride-price*. This important and widespread procedure demands some discussion. Progeny-price is a payment made by the prospective husband (or his father) to the father of the bride. It represents compensation for the loss of her services and the children she will have. It reflects the value which women have as members of a kinship group. In African societies bride-price is often called *lobola*. Typically, it consists of the gift of a number of cattle to the bride's father. Formerly missionaries tried to repress this on the grounds that it degrades a woman to be bought for a few cows. But this view completely missed the point of the transaction which is far from a degrading one. (*a*) It is often found in societies, such as those of East Africa, where cattle are highly venerated and thus sanctify the marriage. (*b*) The higher the *lobola* that is paid, the greater will be the status of the woman and her husband. (*c*) Payment of bride-price legalizes the marriage: without it the couple would not be properly wedded. (*d*) It legitimizes the children and establishes their father's claim to them. (*e*) The amount paid, at least on a first marriage, is usually much more than the young man himself can provide. He borrows, therefore, from his father, brothers and uncles. When the cattle, goats, hoes and other goods are handed over, the bride's father may keep only a small proportion. The rest he uses to repay loans he has previously borrowed in order to pay the progeny-price for his sons' wives. As a result, many people in both families come to be closely bound by reciprocal obligations and have a strong interest in ensuring that the marriage does not break down in divorce. If that happened, the whole transaction might have to be reversed, which would often be impossible. In a few societies sister exchange takes the place of bride-price or exists with it.

Progeny-price may continue to have effects long fter the death of the woman whose marriage began it. A Yurok's social status and his *wergild*, or compensation value for death and injury, depended absolutely on the amount paid for his mother.

A variation on the payment of bride-price is *marriage by service*. This usually occurs at the simpler economic levels and consists in the bridegroom spending two or three years, before or after marriage, serving his parents-in-law by hunting, trapping or tilling their land for them. It is found among the Winnebago tribe of Wisconsin, the Hidatsa of North Dakota, the Chuckchi of Siberia and the African Bemba and Nyakyusa.

The basic principle of bride-price is rooted in kinship ties. It emphasizes that the marriage partners do not stand alone: each is a member of a kin group and their marriage is merely the most conspicuous link in what will henceforth be an alliance of two social groups. In primitive society it can truly be said that you marry your in-laws.

In 1969 this principle was extended when Shaikh Karume imposed an 'export surcharge' of £3,000 on Zanzibari brides going to live with husbands in Tanzania. For various reasons Tanzanian men have attitudes of 'preferential marriage' towards Zanzibari brides and the Shaikh's action expresses the feeling of economic loss when one of these girls leaves the island.

A similar transaction to bride-price is the handing over of a dowry by the bride's father to the groom's family. This is usually found in societies where women are thought of as being an economic liability. In Indian castes practising hypergamy, a substantial dowry may be needed before a high-ranking girl can attract one of the few eligible men of even higher status.

In most societies more or less elaborate ceremonials, often with the exchange of valuable gifts, mark the wedding festivities and all serve the same function: they strengthen the social bonds between two groups of kindred.

The age at marriage varies greatly but is often related to the economic organization of the society. In many primitive groups the parents need to get their children off their hands as soon as possible. The age at marriage is therefore low. It may also be difficult to survive alone, so widows and widowers remarry quickly and often pair with persons much older or younger than themselves. Where hunting skills are hard to learn, men often marry later than among gardeners and farmers. Child betrothal, sometimes with a token or real marriage ceremony, may occur where two lineages want to amalgamate rich possessions, especially land. Among Australian aborigines, where the older men control society, young men wait many years for wives, whereas the girls are taken up early. Even today in rural Ireland men may marry late because the farms are owned and run by their fathers who will not allow a prospective daughter-in-law to enter their lives. Economic reasons underlie this situation.

The rules of exogamy ensure that a husband and wife always come from separate families and households. Where, then, shall they live after marriage? There are five possibilities. (1) They may set up an independent home, in a new locality, of their own choice. This is the common practice with us and is called *neolocal* residence. (2) It may be in the home or locality of the husband's family; (3) of the wife's family; (4) of the husband's mother's brother's family. These are called respectively *patrilocal, matrilocal* and *avunculocal* residence. (5) A few tribes with weak social organization and little property leave the couple to choose between joining the bride's or the groom's family. This is known as *bilocal* residence. Unfortunately, these terms lack precision and much variation is found in the real life arrangements of post-nuptial dwelling. A couple may start with the bride's family, move to the husband's and perhaps let the bride return again to her own people, for a year or two, after a child is born. Avunculocal residence is found on Losap in Micronesia. Here it may be a recent development, from a previous matrilocal system, in response to a heightening of male status. It is practicable owing to the existence of fairly concentrated villages. The urge to adopt it is based on aspects of land use and trade with neighbouring islands within the Caroline group.

G

The place of residence after marriage profoundly effects the new conjugal unit. In patrilocal (sometimes called *virilocal*) groups the wife is a comparative stranger or 'alien' in a community where her husband has daily contact with his parents and brothers who, with their children, form a tightly knit kin group of continuing solidarity. In matrilocal societies the husbands are the strangers whilst their wives, surrounded by their nearest relatives, have a stronger position in the society. But the extent to which these rules affect the partners also largely depends on whether village exogamy is or is not practised.

Patrilocal residence has a general tendency to be linked with patrilineal descent and inheritance, and matrilocal residence with matrilineal descent. This is because the whole organization of marriage is closely involved with economic affairs such as the control of property, above all of land. This correlation is far from absolute, however, and various special features of the social structure may alter it. In the matrilineal Trobriand Islands marriage is patrilocal, but sons of the union usually return to their mother's home village on reaching adult life. Patrilocal residence is, of course, strongly associated with progeny-price: as a Bantu proverb says, 'The children are where the cattle are not'. But it may also imply that the husband has ties, real or magical, with some hunting territory. Similarly matrilocal residence, while reflecting the social structure, may be strongly linked to the economic cultivation of gardens by women. The Bemba and Bisa of Rhodesia are matrilineal but, because tsetse fly prevents the keeping of cattle in their territory and almost all other property is perishable, there is little to inherit. Facts of this kind modify the impact and application of the rules of residence, succession and divorce.

All societies have some means by which unsuccessful marriages can be brought to an end, although many frown on divorce and some make it very difficult to obtain. These are often the ones in which, as we have seen, a substantial progeny-price has been handed over. But even in these divorce is by no means rare. It is sometimes effected by letting the wife be replaced by one of her sisters. In general, it can be said that for most primitive societies the termination of marriage is easy. Often it can be done, with little emotional disturbance, at the whim of either partner. In any of these societies it is made smoother by the ease with which the partners can remarry. In most communities marriage is a secular affair based on social and economic considerations. It seldom has the intensity of religious emotion found in our own society and which largely accounts for the rarity of divorce in Italy or other Catholic countries. This is another factor which makes divorce easy for primitive peoples. On the whole there seems to be little difference between the ease with which men and women can obtain a divorce, despite beliefs to the contrary. Some societies favour the men, others such as the Iroquois and Zuni, favour women. The loading tends to be linked with patrilineal or matrilineal organization but is not invariably so.

Some societies recompense a man if he has to divorce his wife. Among the Vezo Sakalava of Madagascar the first three children that a divorced woman has by her new husband are taken by her former spouse as compensation for the loss of her services and the children she would have borne him.

Grounds for divorce vary from tribe to tribe. Barrenness is almost universal, even where progeny-price is not part of the marriage contract. Cruelty, desertion, adultery and sorcery practised by either partner usually suffice, especially if repeated. But many other grounds exist, including offences by kindred as distinct from spouses. Often little more than mild reciprocal disapproval is needed. Many factors affect the stability of marriage. A Bemba husband stands to gain by a stable union because it helps him to build up the kind of domestic nucleus which, by extension, will eventually lead him to a village headmanship, with its prestige and economic advantages. A secure family background is, of course, highly desirable for young children, but among primitive peoples this is often provided more by the kin group than the father and mother alone. In many cases the 'father' to whom a child looks is his mother's brother, not the physiological father who sometimes has little to do with his offspring. So there is not the same inducement for a maladjusted couple to stay together 'for the sake of the children' as there is with us.

Among the matrilineal Ashanti divorce is very common. The children are then likely to be looked after by their mother's brother – an easy acceptance, since normally nephews are their uncle's heirs. The Ndemba have a high rate because of their practice to divorce a chronically sick spouse, so as to evade the obligations which press heavily on a surviving partner. When their childbearing life is over Gonja women return to their home compounds and the marriage is often dissolved. Among the Somali, infertility is the commonest cause. Termination of trial marriage gives the Tallensi a high rate but subsequent unions are much more stable. It is extremely rare among the Swazi. Among the Yoruba, where women often have a great measure of economic independence, it is they who initiate divorce proceedings. The sororate does not exist there; sex role identity is little stressed; and there are no rigid sexual taboos.

In describing the basic social group, the family, we have looked at a few of the ways in which marriage leads to its formation and continuation. Continuity in a family depends on people tracing descent from parents to children through successive generations. It happens that in most societies a *unilateral* descent and inheritance system is the rule. This means that, for purposes of social grouping, descent is reckoned through the father or through the mother, but not both. The first is called *patrilineal*, the second *matrilineal*. Our own pattern of inheritance, as far as surnames is concerned, is wholly patrilineal as can be seen from the following table (Fig. 36).

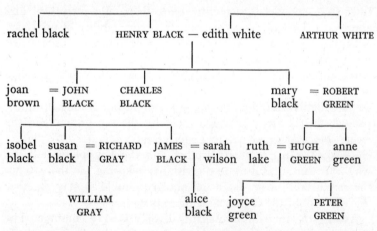

36 Table showing the inheritance of surnames with patrilineal descent.

In a matrilineal descent group the same individuals would have different surnames since, in each case after the first generation,

children would take their mother's name, not that of their father.
See Figure 37.

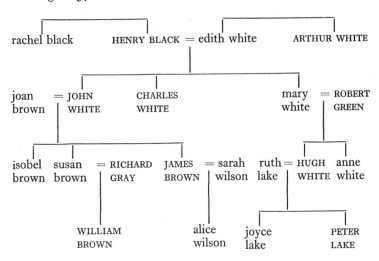

37 Table showing the same persons as in Fig. 36. Here their surnames
are shown in accordance with matrilineal inheritance.

A few peoples trace descent through both parents; these are
called *bilateral* groups. The Cheyenne and Arapaho, typical
buffalo hunters of the American Plains, have recently combined
bilateral descent with matrilocal residence but there is some
evidence that before about 1700 they were eastern agriculturists
living in earthlodge villages and practising matrilineal succession.
Changes of this sort have probably been common in human society.
A *lineage*, which we have already briefly mentioned, is a group
of men and women who trace their descent from a common
ancestor, usually less than ten generations back, through either the
male or the female line. Lineages may or may not have names.
They are often subdivided into so-called maximal and minimal
lineages and various other segments.
A *clan* is similar to a lineage in being a unilateral exogamous
kinship group but it is normally larger. It traces its descent from
some mythological ancestor who lived in a remote past, perhaps
at or near the creation of the world. The myths which tell of its
origin may be highly coloured fantasies but are important in the

social organization of the clan. Sometimes clans are grouped in larger units called *phratries*. These, too, are exogamous. If the society is made up of only two clans or phratries they are known as *moieties* and the tribe is said to have dual organization. These moieties not only provide each other with wives, they also undertake a variety of reciprocal services. Each Choctaw moiety performed the burial ritual for members of the other half. Among the Fox Indians the moieties engaged in contests of dancing, eating, gambling and ball games. Moieties are often residentially separate: some Bororo allot the north side of a village to one half-tribe, the south side to the other.

The number of clans in a phratry or tribe is very variable. In North America, the Omaha had ten patrilineal clans, the Mohawk had three matrilineal ones; the Cherokee had seven called Wolf, Deer, Bird, Red Paint, Blue Paint, Wild Potato and Twister. The Tlingit and Haida had more than fifty clans each. The great African nation of the Baganda has about three dozen patrilineal clans or *kika*, most of which have well-defined and important political duties. Some clans in the dense populations of Africa contain many thousands of members, all of whom, as a social fiction, are related. The way in which clan membership is determined may be very complicated in Australia. A simple example is seen in the Karadjeri tribe. This is divided into four sections, of which the Panaka and Paldjeri make one patrilineal moiety, the Burung and Karimba another. Their marriage and affiliation system may be represented as:

$$\begin{array}{c} \rightarrow \text{PANAKA} = \text{BURUNG} \leftarrow \\ \rightarrow \text{KARIMBA} = \text{PALDJERI} \leftarrow \end{array}$$

In this a Karimba man must marry a Paldjeri woman and their children will belong to the Burung group; a Paldjeri man marries a Karimba woman to produce Panaka children; a Panaka man marries a Burung woman, their children being Paldjeri; and a Burung man must marry a Panaka woman and their children will be Karimba.

The clan system is intimately woven into many aspects of tribal life. Apart from its regulation of marriage, through the rule of exogamy, it serves the general function of providing mutual aid and security on a basis of kinship. Social ties within the clan are so close that not only will clansmen unite to support each other but vengeance for an offence committed by one clansman, murder for example, may be taken on any other member of the clan even if he is innocent. This concern with social solidarity and collective liability endows the clan with legal powers, the operation of which may be informally exercised through public opinion or more formally enforced by a headman or council of elders. Political decisions and powers, war-making for example, are sometimes vested in one clan of a tribe. The Warrior clan of the Winnebago Indians led the tribal war parties. The Trobriand Islanders and many African groups have a royal clan from which the chief always comes. Especially among advanced food-producing societies, clans have control of property and land, and organize trading or other economic exchanges. They have, too, important religious functions which vary from tribe to tribe. Often each clan will have specific ceremonies to perform for the benefit of the whole society. One of the commonest features of a clan is its possession of a *totem*.

This is usually some species of animal, mammal, bird, reptile or insect, or a plant. Occasionally it may be inanimate, such as a rock, water, thunder or other natural feature. Totemism is difficult to define precisely. Its essence is an association or quality which is felt to exist between the group of people who own the totem and the animal or plant which it represents. Primitive peoples show great variety in the way they act out totemic beliefs. Among the commonest attributes of Totemism we find the following: the human group is named from its totem; the origin of the totem is explained in elaborate myths; the people believe they are descended from the totem, which was partly human as well as animal or plant; magico-religious rituals are often connected with totems and may re-enact the origin myth; people are forbidden to kill or eat their totem species; carvings or other representations of the totem are commonly found and may be highly venerated; totemic groups are usually exogamous. Any of these features of totemism may be absent from a group. The Seneca Indians of the Iroquoian Confederation were divided into two moieties. The first consisted of four clans having as their totems the bear, wolf, turtle and beaver respectively. The second also had four clans whose totems were the deer, heron, snipe and hawk. None of the clans were tabooed from eating their totem, nor did they have any religious rites centred upon them. The four clans of Tikopia could also freely eat their totem plant but unlike those of the five Iroquoian tribes they were not exogamous. One of these tribes, the Mohawk, also had a turtle clan which included a chief with the title Haienh-watha. It was a great sixteenth-century holder of this office who gave rise to the later legends associated with the hero whose name was corrupted to 'Hiawatha'.

Totems are not limited to clans. They may be associated with moieties or with individuals. In the Hunter River tribes of Australia, they were divided by sex: the bat was sacred to men, the woodpecker to women. Other forms and borderline cases exist but cannot be described here. The importance of totemism is shown by its integration with social structure, tribal art, linguistic nuances, magic, religion, law, morals and much else in the lives of primitive groups.

Lineages and clans are unilateral groups of consanguineous kin. Another important social grouping is the *extended* (or *joint*) *family*, but its structure is quite different from a clan because it has an organization which includes affinal kin. An extended family may be patrilineal or matrilineal. If patrilineal it normally consists of a core of genealogically related men with their wives, unmarried daughters, and the wives who have married into it from other groups. It does not include daughters who have left it through marriage. Matrilineal joint families are correspondingly structured around a core of genealogically related women. As in all such social groups, considerable variety is found in practice. The Yugoslav *zadruga* is an extended family. In a South Serbian one, eleven families lived in a twenty-room house. They were joint owners of a large tract of land which made them economically self-sufficient, a distinctive feature of this kind of grouping. The work of the community was partly specialized: six women baked and cooked; eight did the spinning, weaving and clothes-making; five men looked after the animals; one made shoes. Unlike clans, whose members may be widely scattered, an extended family is always a local unit. Although extended families may be, to some degree, in economic competition with each other, the fact that any one of them is probably united with several others by marriage serves to integrate and stabilize the societies in which they are found.

7 SOCIETY (II)

Further aspects of living together

Local organization, house patterns, *esprit de corps*, prescribed behaviour, individual and society, status and role again, age-sets, clubs and fraternities, *rites de passage*, slavery, stratified societies, segmented societies.

So far the aspects of society which we have discussed have been chiefly those concerning people's relationships to each other in various groups of kindred: in family, lineage or clan. But other social bonds exist and there is more to society than social structure.

It is uncertain to what extent persons have a territory sense comparable to that of robins and many other species of birds or mammals. There is no doubt that many tribes, clans and families claim to own an area of land, or at least the right to exploit it, and they jealously resist intrusion by strangers. The way in which primitive groups occupy territory is an important aspect of their social cohesion and is spoken of as their *local organization*.

Local groups vary greatly in size. A most important one to which we have already referred is the *tribe*. Tribes are groups of people who usually speak a common language or dialect; they live in a fairly well defined territory, and share a culture which is moderately homogeneous. Tribes are not exogamous nor are they usually kinship groups. They may consist of a few surviving persons from once larger bands, such as are found in many American and Australian tribal remnants, or they may be large units such as the Ibo tribe of Nigeria which numbers about four million people, and could almost be ranked as a nation if it were not for its weak and diffused political coherence. When of this size they are always divided into sub-tribes or smaller local groups. The size of these groups partly depends on the type of economy which is practised. Simple food gatherers and nomadic pastoralists always consist of small units. Advanced agriculturists may live in large and densely populated communities. The geographical background is important. Mountain peoples, such as those of New Guinea or the Andes, often have tiny villages perched on ledges or squeezed into narrow ravines; spacious plains living, as in

Cochin or Nigeria, encourages dense populations provided soil and climate are favourable.

Village patterns closely reflect social patterns. Types of dwelling, too, are interrelated with the organization and functions of society and kinship systems. The widely scattered and separate log and mud houses of Navajo pastoralists reflect their loose system of social organization and bolster their individualistic attitudes. The Plains Indian tipis not only expressed the mobility and partial nomadism of these tribes, they also emphasized in their camp arrangement the structure of the group. The great communal stone and masonry houses of the Pueblo Indians are very different. One at Pueblo Bonito in New Mexico had about five hundred rooms and might have sheltered a couple of thousand persons. The pueblos were defensive forts as well as dwellings and their outer walls were blank surfaces, doorless and windowless. Entrance was by ladder down the smoke hole, and all windows and doors faced inwards on to the courtyard where their ritual dances and rich ceremonial life was concentrated. These people turned their backs, literally and symbolically, upon the hostile world. Their great buildings formed a compact, tightly integrated whole, where families lived in congested intimacy. Functionally, this reinforced the intensely co-operative pattern of their social structure, but it also seems to have bred a tendency to excessive touchiness, bickering and fear of witchcraft.

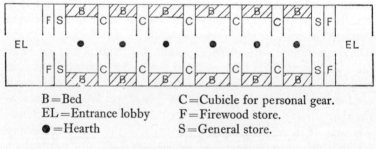

B = Bed   C = Cubicle for personal gear.
EL = Entrance lobby   F = Firewood store.
● = Hearth   S = General store.

38 Plan of an Iroquois longhouse.

The typical Iroquois dwelling was the longhouse (Fig. 38). This was a rectangular structure which might be 30 feet wide and as much as 100 yards long. Doors were at each end and a central passageway went the entire length of the house. Off this, on each side, were open compartments about 12 to 15 feet square. Each of these was occupied by a conjugal family. Between each pair of cubicles a cooking fire or hearth lay in the central corridor. These longhouses were owned by a lineage of related women, the head of the house being one of the older and most influential of them. Her daughters, their husbands and their children lived in the building. Often her sisters and their conjugal families, and also the families of her married granddaughters, would be included. The house expressed the matrilocal pattern of a society structured in matrilineal clans. Between the different conjugal families there was less suppressed tension than among the Pueblo peoples. Living was close and intimate, as with the Pueblos, but unlike them an entire village was not concentrated into a single building. An Iroquois tribe was scattered in a number of villages, each of which had several or many longhouses. Even more important in reducing tensions within the longhouse was the fact that the Iroquoians were persistent warriors who could release their internal tensions in aggressive forays against traditional enemies. This integration of house types with social structure and cultural attitudes is emphasized by the collapse of Iroquois longhouse living, and its replacement by small log houses, under the impact of the white colonization of their country which disrupted their social pattern. It is also well shown in Trobriand villages. Here the dominant structures are not dwelling houses but *bwayma*, the elaborate huts in which the annual yam crop is stored. They stand conspicuously raised on foundation stones, their size and ornateness geared to the social status of the owner. Their intricate design and the care with which they are built reflects the importance of yams, not only as a staple crop but as a focus of much social ceremonial. By contrast, Trobriand living houses are rather shoddy structures. Their crowded placing and lack of foundation piers expresses the native fear of sorcery: little room is left for sorcerers to prowl between or beneath these dwellings.

The most important fact about a society is not that people are gathered together in one place but that they have developed certain psychological attitudes and responses to each other. They feel an overall unity of interests, an *esprit de corps*, which is based on years of living in the same tribe or village, working and playing together, gossiping and squabbling, and getting to know each

other's personalities so that a man can predict the reactions of his
neighbour. This gives a sense of security. You may not like the
family in the next igloo, grass hut or tree house, but at least you
know more or less how they will behave in any situation.

There seem to be several factors which cause this sense of social
unity to develop.

Firstly there is *living together*. If people are closely grouped on
a Polynesian atoll, in a forest clearing or along the banks of a small
stream, they cannot escape getting to know each other well. There
are few occasions when unpredictable behaviour disrupts their
feeling of security together and each man knows within quite
narrow limits where he stands with each of his neighbours, though
it must be conceded that only a minority of societies are small
enough to be truly face-to-face, intergossiping units throughout
their whole extent. Indeed, a characteristic of many societies is
that they have evolved precise patterns of behaviour between
individuals so that unexpected and emotionally tense situations
shall not arise. We have already briefly looked at these customs.

These prescribed behaviour patterns take various forms. One
of the commonest is that certain relatives must avoid each other.
There are many tribes in which a man must have no contact with
his mother-in-law. If he sees her coming through the village he
may have to take a roundabout path to avoid her; if she enters his
house he has to leave; or he may be unable to eat any, or some
kinds of, food prepared by her. Among the Galla a man was not
allowed to mention the name of his wife's mother; among the
Baganda he was permitted neither to see nor speak to her. Similar
rules often exist between a brother and sister once they have
grown up. In much of Melanesia they may be forbidden to eat or
to talk together or they may merely have to avoid certain topics
of conversation. Women may have similar prohibitions concerning
their husband's father.

Another curious but widely spread form of behaviour is known
as the *joking relationship*. It was well developed among the Crow
Indians of North America, the Tswana of Botswana, the Lozi of
Barotzeland and many other tribes. It takes the form of an obliga-
tion to tease and play tricks on certain relatives, such as a man's
maternal uncle or his brothers-in-law who are younger than
himself. The jokes are of a kind that would normally give great
offence, but where the joking relationship exists the victim is not

allowed to display annoyance. He must accept even abuse with good grace.

These two customs, the one of respectful avoidance and the other of boisterous familiarity, are so often found in association that they can be considered as complementary ways of achieving an identical social function – the elimination of conflict among near kindred. The avoidance rules usually involve the relationships of a man or woman with someone in the previous generation; the joking rules commonly operate within one generation or between grandparent and grandchild. Marriage produces a temporary disturbance in two families that have previously been jogging along in some sort of equilibrium. The most obvious points of tension which a marriage creates are centred on the relationship of the new husband to his wife's mother, that is, the two persons most closely impinging on the bride. Avoidance patterns vary but they all serve a similar purpose. As the marriage progresses and the two kindred groups settle down to readjust their relationships, the avoidance rules are sometimes allowed to lapse. Joking familiarity serves to avert domestic hostility by canalizing it into socially acceptable and predictable forms. It symbolizes conflict and at the same time takes the sting out of it. Among the Tswana, it is practised by cross cousins, between whom marriage is much favoured. One reason given for this by the natives is that it makes for tolerance and indulgence between husband and wife, thus helping to ensure a stable marriage.

Even in our own society we have similar standardized rules of behaviour, though they tend to be more in evidence with strangers and they are only weakly related to social structure, not at all to kinship organization. An especially uncertain time is at the moment when we are first introduced to a new acquaintance. Our conventional 'How do you do?', perhaps followed by some platitude about the weather, is a useful way to open conversation in an exploratory, non-committal fashion without the risk of starting too soon on a subject that might cause embarrassment or offence.

Australian aborigines who do not know each other have to establish, by enquiry, their relative social positions and status as soon as they meet. Only when this has been done does each know what is his proper behaviour towards the other.

Mutual adjustment of this kind is one of the ways in which people conform to social pressures and learn to fill an acceptable role in society. They learn to curb self-assertiveness within permissible bounds and this, in turn, leads to some sacrifice of personal interests for the benefit of the community. In return for this acquiescence and conformity, the community sustains its members when each needs help or support. It is an efficient way of imposing a measure of social control over the selfish drives of individuals.

But although persons are thus dominated and shaped by their society, they are not obliterated by it. They may actually change or mould it as well as being moulded by it. They may introduce a new religion as Knox and Luther did in Western Europe and Akhenaten in Egypt, or a new political and social system as Kemal Atatürk did in Turkey, or a new system of hospital nursing and administration as Florence Nightingale brought about.

It is through these efforts of individuals, as well as by common consent, that societies change and adapt themselves for survival. If no change took place their old patterns of behaviour might become a liability when the outside world changed.

For example, the prejudice of Victorian society against the employment of gentlewomen in industry became potentially dangerous during World War I when all available labour was needed in munitions factories and for help in furthering the war effort. In this case the Victorian pattern yielded to the new pressures. Australian clans have sometimes been faced with a situation in which almost all game, except for their totem animal which they are not allowed to eat, has disappeared from their hunting territory. The choice then became one of starving to death or of adapting to the new conditions by breaking the taboo. In some small Australian groups, in which a man had to choose a wife from a limited number of women outside his own clan, it occasionally happened that not a single permitted woman was available. In these circumstances he must take a tabooed woman if he wanted to marry and raise a family. Unless the group was prepared to make the concession it would soon be on the way to extinction. Usually the concession is made, but the offending couple will be given a beating and temporarily expelled from the tribe as a token of formal disapproval, which itself reassures the rest that they are virtuous conformists. In this way biological adaptation is achieved at the same time as tribal ideals are preserved intact.

The patterns of behaviour in any society are almost always taken for granted by its members. This is especially true among primitives. Arapesh women normally carry much heavier loads on their heads than men. They explain this by saying that women's heads are harder and stronger – which, of course, is not true. In Dr. Johnson's time women as well as men meekly believed in the doctrine of women's mental inferiority. In England today class differences, fox hunting, capitalism, imprisonment and mini-skirts are still accepted without question by most, but by no means all, members of our society: in a hundred years time (much less for mini-skirts!) none of these features may be more than a faded memory.

Of the many patterns of behaviour that are found in large societies only a few are known to most people. A miner is likely to know nothing of court etiquette; a member of the Church of England may have no idea what to do in a synagogue or at a Catholic Mass; an army officer may know little of the intricate ways in which girls in a boarding school behave towards each other.

Notice how closely this reflects what we have already said about the existence of 'sub-cultures'. It illustrates the intimate relationship of culture and society.

As we have seen, everybody has to fill certain positions in society which are called statuses and has certain roles to carry out. These are, in effect, patterns of behaviour. A man may have some duties from his status as a father, other duties as a taxpayer, others because he is a barrister and still others because he is an M.P. and a Catholic.

Some of our statuses come to us automatically as a result of our sex, our hereditary position, our age and much else. Thus, with no effort on our part we may be baronets, uncles, members of an Indian caste, daughters in a family of suburban Jews or Tikopian grandmothers. These are called *ascribed* statuses. Others may come to us as a result of our own efforts. We become millionaires, shamans, lawyers, sponge divers and so on. These are known as *achieved* statuses. Most of the statuses concerned with the humdrum affairs of everyday living devolve on us as a result of our sex, age, family position, class or clan membership: they are ascribed. Societies in which achievable statuses are plentiful offer rich scope for full participation by their members. They benefit by allowing people to find their most efficient niches and occupations as a result of competition, social striving and internal social mobility. Societies with an unduly high proportion of ascribed statuses may be inefficient to the extent that people are forced to play roles for which they are not suited. On the other hand, the individual may be more relaxed in these less competitive societies; he is not frustrated by failing to achieve a status at which it would never occur to him to aim.

Sometimes the behaviour demanded by the different patterns in which a person is involved may put conflicting duties on him. Situations of this kind should not arise too often because of the strain they impose on individuals and through them on society as a whole. When they do occur they are the very stuff of drama. Examples are, the Scottish laird who finds himself bound by the laws of hospitality to be host to a man who has turned out to be an hereditary enemy from a hostile clan; or Brutus caught between the demands of the friendship he owed to Julius Caesar and his patriotic allegiance to the State of Rome.

In many societies, especially the extremely complex ones, group conflicts are common and may take the form of quarrels between different sects, different economic and industrial organizations, urban and rural populations, and many others. In our own society we need only think of the diverse attitudes that people have towards gambling, alcohol, divorce, equal pay for women, corporal punishment or farm subsidies. These attitudes show the diversity of ideals and interests that are found. They also show that, at least in part, they cut across age, occupational, class or religious groupings.

Many different ways of organizing society have developed, some of which are more likely than others to encourage group solidarities or group antagonisms. We have already seen that wherever the clan system exists the members of one clan are likely to form a very close-knit unit against outsiders. In many parts of Africa, as amongst the Sherente of Brazil and elsewhere, the men are organized into *age-sets*. At a certain age all eligible youths begin a period of graduated initiation ceremonies which may last for many years. Every few years the members of one set are up-graded to the next, and to the end of their lives the men who originally began as a single age-grade will feel linked by bonds of special loyalty and solidarity to each other. This is a primitive equivalent of 'the old school tie' attitude that can still be found in England.

In groups such as the Nandi of Kenya, the Swazi of Botswana or the Nyakyusa of Lake Nyasa, age classes are well developed and serve to promote social integration and efficiency. Each age group is strongly aware of its identity and its position in society. Members of each set advance together throughout life. They start as young boys awaiting initiation, become unmarried warriors, then married men and finally tribal elders. At every stage the men of one set feel a special sense of *esprit de corps*, a unity and mutual dependence which knits them closely together. Age-sets help to smooth the transition that a boy must make when he leaves his own primary family and starts a family of his own. The warrior age groups also functioned as efficient fighting regiments in many African tribes. They are sometimes used as the basis of work gangs.

Clubs, fraternities and the so-called *'secret societies'* are other groupings which may be important in the integration, or segmentation, of society as a whole. Their common characteristic is that they are associations of people which are not based on kinship, but are voluntary. They have a limited membership within the larger society, they have their own formal structure and inspire a feeling of exclusive 'togetherness' in their members. In primitive communities clubs such as these are usually for men only.

The Yoruba of West Africa have a secret fraternity called the Ogboni. Its members are important family and village headmen. The Ogboni functions chiefly as a political organization which exercises great power over the chief. It also protects the interests of its members and takes secret 'legal' action against anyone who may conflict with it. The Yoruba also have two great religious societies, the Oro and the Egungan. Clubs of this sort are very common. They are useful as mutual aid societies, as brakes on the power of despotic or arrogant chiefs, as controllers of social behaviour. But they are often also homicidal and cannibalistic. Their members may be corrupted by the lust for power and, as with the famous Ekkpe or Leopard fraternities, they terrorize society for their own purposes.

Among the Pueblo tribes, fraternities are wholly religious, magical and ceremonial in their function. Among the Plains Indians the clubs are often called 'military societies', though they did not act primarily as regiments or fighting units. Some, such as the Crow Tobacco Society, were magico-religious in their

H

activities, others were partly economic, partly military and hunting organizations. Membership of the ungraded clubs of the
Crow, Cheyenne, Kiowa and other tribes was open to all adult
males. In the graded clubs of the Mandan, Hidatsa and Blackfoot
a prestige hierarchy was present through which a man could
advance only if he had the right qualifications of age, gift-giving
or ability to purchase a higher rank.

Among the Plains tribes, as also in Dahomey, a few women's
clubs occurred.

In Australia and throughout Oceania, men's clubs are common
and are roughly similar in function to the ones described already
(Plate VIII). An exceptional one was the *arioi* of the Society
Islands. It was open to men and women and was strongly rank
graded. Its chief function was to provide entertainments such as
songs, dancing, drama and games. Its members had to be childless
and whenever children were born to them these infants were
immediately killed. It is not easy to interpret the social significance
of the *arioi*. In its partial reversal of normal social behaviour,
which also included the lampooning of sacred chiefs, it seems to
have been a kind of 'Lord of Misrule' and to have canalized social
aggressions, boredom and frustration into mostly harmless directions. But it also fulfilled magico-religious functions when it
invoked the god Oro-i-te-tea-moe.

Almost all voluntary associations of this kind have more or less
elaborate initiation ceremonies. The ones which are graded in a
hierarchy usually impose substantial economic demands on the
up-going members. Here, too, there is a general tendency for
these members not only to rank high in the association but also to
be high outside it, in political power, social rank and wealth.

Voluntary associations also exist in our own society: freemasonry
is one example, the notorious Ku Klux Klan is another. These
tend to differ from primitive associations in that membership is
secret, as well as the activities of the members. Among primitives
only the activities are normally secret.

Initiation ceremonies, where men or women pass from one
grade or status to another, are often called by the French term
rites de passage or 'passage rites'. Puberty ceremonies marking the
transition from childhood to adolescence are of this kind. So, too,
are rites which celebrate the attainment of married status, parent-
hood and other statuses. They all have the effect of defining with

some precision the position which a person holds in the community at any time. They are another method of giving a sense of
social orientation.

These passage rites must be seen as being, above all, the
recognition by society that a change – sometimes a physiological
change – has taken place in a person. This biological change may
have occurred quite a long time previously, but not until the
appropriate rite has been performed is it accepted as a social fact.
In ancient Greece a man was not thought of as 'officially' dead
until he had been buried with the appropriate ceremony. To omit
the passage rites for the occasion was considered a great calamity:
it left the corpse with no proper status as a dead man.

Because, in primitive societies, men almost always take a more
prominent part in ceremonial life than women, initiation rites are
usually far more elaborate for males than females. Circumcision is
the commonest form of these rites but hundreds of others exist.
Many involve severe or repeated physical suffering and they are
often designed to leave a permanent visible mark. Tattooing, the
production of extensive weals and scars, or the amputation of
fingers are of this kind. Especially when the novices are young,
their kinsfolk often play a prominent part in the ritual. They may
support and encourage the youth during his ordeal and may
themselves suffer various disabilities. This kin involvement is yet
another example of social cohesion and shows how special events
reflect the social structure of the group.

In our own society various *rites de passage* can be found. The
religious ceremonies of baptism, confirmation and ordination are
of this nature. So, too, are the rituals associated with dubbing a
knight, installing the grand-master of a freemason's lodge,
graduation day at a university, 'blooding' someone after their first
fox hunt or, at a very light-hearted level, the pranks and horseplay
aimed at ships' passengers when they cross the equator for the
first time.

We should always bear in mind that the basic function of social
organization is to make it easier for people to live together. If there
were no rules, habits or customs to which people had to conform
the result would be chaos. Even situations that at a first glance
seem wholly unpleasant may have compensations for the persons
involved in them.

Slavery is an example. We are used to thinking of a slave as a pitiable creature, denied all rights and freedoms, and subjected to every cruelty or oppression at the lightest whim of his owner. In practice slavery hardly ever works like this. Slaves are valuable – in some societies very valuable and difficult to obtain – so a slave owner will look after this human property as carefully as he can. He will feed and house his slaves with care; he will not overwork them; he will keep them as contented as possible by allowing them to marry among themselves and by giving them as many privileges as possible. In some groups, especially among the nations of West Africa, it would not be easy at a casual glance to distinguish between slave and freeman. Sometimes their children were regarded as freeborn.

In tribes such as the Yoruba of Nigeria the king had many slaves who rose to great eminence, power and wealth. Often they were highly valued because they were the only persons close to him on whose loyalty a chief could rely. They frequently stood between him and the hostile schemings of his freeborn relatives. In these circumstances, although slaves were theoretically without civil rights, they were an élite group and nothing might be more catastrophic for one of them than manumission – his release from comfortable bondage into a world where he was cast adrift on his own without the protection of his overlord.

Not all, or even the majority, of slaves had it as good as these great court officials, some of whom even had slaves of their own. But no matter what his level was, any slave at least had the social security of knowing his exact position in society. In many places, if a man was born a slave, he knew he would live and die a slave, together with his children after him. This may have meant physical discomfort but it was social and psychological security.

By contrast, in societies such as our own or that of the U.S.A., a man has no such security. He is tempted by the glittering promise that anyone born in a log cabin can become President or at least a millionaire. It is true that any *one* can . . . to the inevitable exclusion of 150 million others who cannot. Yet these others may have set their hearts on achieving the promised goal. Their inevitable failure leads them to endless social insecurity as they struggle along, with sourness and frustration as a result.

What has just been said about slavery applies to other classes as well. In many societies where rank is hereditary it is no doubt pleasant to be born into the nobility or aristocracy, though duties and obligations, often onerous, are universally found to off-set privileges. The middle or lower classes may be less comfortably endowed; they may face harder work, less freedom and more poverty. But so long as a man knows what his position is, as he would in a feudal society, he can feel secure enough without being perpetually tormented by the hope of unrealizable dreams of improving his lot.

Societies in which marked differences of class or rank are conspicuous are called *stratified societies*. Their social organization consists of a powerful centralized authority often based on the control of land, with an administrative machine. Many of the Bantu-speaking populations of Africa are of this type. They consist of a chief, sub-chiefs, district and village headmen, and a parallel establishment of courtiers, councillors, deputies and legal officials. Their duties and privileges are clearly defined and carefully graded. Everyone knows his place in the social system.

A similar pattern of stratified society existed in Tonga, and elsewhere in Polynesia, where the sanctity and secular authority of the leading aristocrats was reinforced by kinship ties between them, ties which were systematically developed by rules of class endogamy. Social stratification can be efficiently maintained by endogamous marriage, so the two conditions are commonly found together, even when not formally referred to as such.

A different type of social organization is found in *segmented societies*. Many Amerindian, most Melanesian and all Australian tribes are of this kind. So, too, are the Eskimo. In segmented societies each small local band, whether tribe, clan, or extended family, forms a self-contained, self-controlled unit. It will be governed by a few respected elders or councillors and will be held together mostly by bonds of kinship or clan allegiance. For special occasions several of these autonomous units may combine but they rarely do so under the control of any centralized authority.

This account of a few of the ways in which society is bound together is extremely simplified. There are many more patterns, and variations on them, that cannot be dealt with here. It is enough to repeat once again that these patterns, through which social cohesion is attained, have developed in response to a biological need . . . the need of men to live together in organized, smoothly integrated groups.

8 RELIGION AND MAGIC

Man's comfort in distress

Animism, magic and religion, increase ceremonies, ancestor worship, animatism, *mana*, *orenda*, *shamans* and priests, mythology, taboo, *cargo cults*.

Religion is one of the most important aspects of human activity. It is also one of the most difficult to define. All societies have some system of belief in supernatural forces but the range of variation is so vast that no definition in terms of any one of these systems is adequate. Perhaps the best we can say is that religion simply is a belief in the supernatural, together with the mental attitudes and patterns of behaviour that follow from it. As in much else, the earlier anthropologists used to ask an 'origin' question: 'How did religion (or some specific manifestation of it) begin?'

Consider *animism*, which is the belief in intangible, disembodied beings such as ghosts, wandering souls, demons or other spirits which are individual and specifically associated with definite places. They may inhabit streams, glens, rocks, trees or animals and they have power to help or injure humans. Their aid may be sought or their wrath placated by anyone who knows the proper way to approach them. Many explanations of their origin have been put forward. The mocking voice of an echo, hazy reflections in a pool or the growl of thunder may have suggested to primitive man that strange beings haunted the hills, the tarns or the skies. Hallucinations from fever or from poisonous plants may have produced visions of insubstantial creatures. We cannot know, but the first dawning of these notions was surely very ancient. Cave artists of the Old Stone Age have left scenes which strongly hint at magic rituals intended to bring them success in hunting. From a still earlier age, Neandertal burials have been found where the corpse had been covered with ochre and accompanied by grave goods, suggesting a belief in an after-life. Perhaps the first faint stirrings of a sense of the supernatural or the spooky are coeval with the emergence of man himself. Even chimpanzees have been observed to show a feeling of awe when confronted by a strange object.

Explanations of this kind have little value. They are 'pseudo-historical', the result of unverifiable speculation. Today we ask different questions: 'What function does religion play in the culture of any society? How does it serve individual and collective needs? In what way does each of its elements help social cohesion and make life easier to live?'

Many writers draw a sharp distinction between religion and *magic*. They point out that religion operates through the medium of spirits or deities and its results are dependent on their goodwill; it is a shared activity; it is publicly approved; and, often, it consists in acts of worship which have no special purpose other than the worship itself. By contrast, magic always has some definite end in view; it produces direct or automatic results for anyone who knows the correct ritual or spell; it is independent of help from the gods; it is usually private and secret; and it is often malicious and antisocial. But in many cases this clear-cut distinction is unjustified. It is better to think of magico-religious activities and beliefs in which the two attitudes are variously mingled according to individual circumstances.

Homeopathic or *imitative magic* is based on the assumption that if two objects or acts resemble each other in shape, colour, smell or other quality they must be related to each other and that anything done to one will affect the other. When Zuni priests roll large stones around their *kivas*, the rock-hewn rooms in which they perform many of their rituals, the rumble of the boulders imitates the noise of thunder clouds. By this resemblance they hope to bring rain for their maize crops. This is undoubtedly magic, but it is socially approved and performed by a body of priests so it is also religion. *Black magic* is an expression sometimes applied to practices which are designed to bring injury or death to someone. Black magic and imitative magic are not mutually exclusive terms, however. Both can be applied to the incantation of a Dobuan which is intended to destroy his victim's face by the horrible disease *gangosa*. He aims to do this by reciting a spell which describes how the hornbill bird rends the bark of a tree in just the way that his enemy's face shall be ravaged by the infection.

Magico-religious practices are of bewildering diversity but they are never isolated oddities. In every society they form a system which is integrated with the total cultural pattern. Their function, which is achieved in many ways, is to develop feelings of group unity on the basis of collectively shared sentiments, to engender psychological comfort and security by filling gaps in practical knowledge and to give confidence in difficult or dangerous situations. They are much found, therefore, in situations which are tense with anxiety or peril. For instance, some Polynesians have elaborate fishing magic when they go out on the dangerous waters of the open ocean but none for the sheltered calm of the lagoons. Even with us the average clerk, in a steady Civil Service pensionable job, is not much given to what we call 'superstition'. By contrast, professional gamblers, air pilots, sailors and actors – all in precarious and uncertain occupations – are often very superstitious. Many are reluctant to begin a new enterprise without a battery of mascots, magic tokens and lucky charms.

Australian natives perform many magico-religious rituals which are intended to ensure the abundance of different kinds of animals and plants, especially those which are important foods. These are known as *increase ceremonies* and are usually the 'property' of a single clan. To the participants they give a sense of social solidarity and security. They play a major part in the economic life of the group; they reflect the system of clan organization; their performance by the old men mirrors the political set-up of the society; and their associated mythology is closely linked to their totemic beliefs. In this way they are interwoven with the total culture.

Increase ceremonies are communal activities but private magical practices also reflect cultural organization. The Cherokee Indians of North Carolina made great use of love magic. A complicated series of charms would be used by a young man to engage the help of certain spirits; to enhance his own attractiveness and status; to make his clan rivals ridiculous and unattractive; and to make the girl he loved feel lonely and yearn for a husband from his clan. This complex of charms reflects Cherokee clan organization, the familiarity or joking relationship (in denigrating rivals), attitudes towards status, and kinship principles of preferential marriage.

The extent to which people are involved in magico-religious activity varies from one society to another. We have referred to animism, the belief in ghosts, spirits, elves, fairies, goblins, devils or gods. It is a belief which seems to be universal. A special form of animism is *ancestor worship*, which is well developed in Africa and China. It reflects kinship patterns and has a powerful function in promoting family unity. Among the Tanala, a Madagascan tribe of rice-growers, an important social unit is the extended family. The founders of these families were worshipped by all their patrilineal descendants and the desire to become such a founder was a powerful incentive for men to break away from their paternal group, though few were able to do this. So strong was the feeling about ancestors that the Tanala family was divided into two groups, the living and the dead, each equally real in native thought. Death was imagined as little more than a change of residence. At his funeral ceremony a dead Tanala was told of his new status; he was introduced to his ancestors, who were asked to treat him well; his marriage in life was dissolved and he was told he could remarry among the shades. Ancestors were invited to the feasts of the living; they were given food to take home to dead ancestors who had been absent from the feast owing to business or illness; they were consulted on many matters and could visit or be visited in dreams. In short, they were ever present in the native mind.

Another way of conceiving the supernatural is called *animatism*. Again a non-material force or power is imagined but this time it takes the form of a diffuse, non-specific, all-pervading spiritual essence which is often called *mana*, from a Melanesian word. This force permeates all things, living and dead. It may be drawn on as a source of miraculous power by those who know the formulae or it may be inherent in them. Unlike animism, with which it may coexist, the concept of animatism is far from universal. It is widespread in Oceania. There, a spear is sharp because it possesses *mana*, the *mana* of a fish-net brings in a good haul (Plate IX); coconuts grow, a dance is beautiful, chiefs are powerful and priests holy because *mana* pervades them. A force of such potency is full of danger. Such an intensity of *mana* is concentrated in some Polynesian chiefs that they must be carried over ground belonging to other people lest the touch of their feet should make it too holy to grow crops.

Animatism is also common in North America where the supernatural force is sometimes known as *manito* or *orenda*. In many of the tribes when a young American Indian was growing up the most important event of his life took place. This was the quest for his 'vision', a mystical experience which was destined to influence his entire future. It was the custom for the young man to go alone, or with a trusted helper, into some wild and dangerous place.

There he would endure privations, hunger or torture and reduce himself to a state of hallucination in which *manito* would enter into him. It was often brought by the vision of a bear, a beautiful woman or a bird who would for ever after be a kind of guardian spirit to him. But his actual source of power was from the all-pervading forces of nature. From them, through his 'vision', he would acquire his prowess as a warrior, his luck as a hunter or his skill as a medicine man. If he killed other warriors their *orenda* was thought to be added to his own just as a Marquesan Islander absorbed the *mana* of the enemies he slew.

Many examples of the vision are recorded. They show, yet again, the integration of different aspects of culture. The power, or 'medicine', derived from them always augments or bestows qualities which have practical or prestige value in Amerindian society. The solitary, self-inflicted ordeals of the vision quest reflect the aggressive and individualistic nature of these peoples, and their striving for status as fearless warriors. A man who failed to acquire *orenda* was handicapped throughout life, so dominant in native thought was this experience.

A feature of magico-religious beliefs in primitive peoples is their broad uniformity within any one society. Most persons subscribe to an identical system of belief, however much they vary in punctilious observance of it. This contrasts with the diversity in complex Western civilizations. Within Christianity the average high Anglican is of a different social class from the average Salvationist; the average Quaker has a different standard of education from the typical Jehovah's Witness. In the U.S.A. religious sects are sensitive indicators of social status, economic level and, frequently in a town, of residential locality.

Other differences exist between primitive peoples and advanced civilizations. *Ethics*, the rules dealing with moral principles and proper conduct, is usually less emphasized by primitive religions. This is because they are less organized: relations between gods and their worshippers are personal rather than institutional. The advanced religions place great emphasis on ethics and codes of moral conduct but many variations are found amongst them. The Hindu practises asceticism, or self-denial (Plate xi). Mohammedanism inclines more to puritan ethic: that is, it seeks to apply asceticism to others. It is, too, only the advanced religions which are proselytizing and seek to convert any or all other groups to their own doctrinal systems. They aim to be world religions and, at least in the past, have denied the truth of any creeds but their own. Often they focus their rituals on one outstanding personality such as a Buddha or a Mahomet. Primitive religions have virtually no interest in winning converts. The advanced religions usually promise their believers an after life with some sort of immortality. This is rare with the primitives who mostly have little conception of an eternal life and who see death as a transition to a rather vague existence where the ghosts of the departed may linger for a while before gradually fading to oblivion. However, they attach great importance to the control of these ghosts as long as they are around. Occasionally the idea of an after life is phrased as a belief in reincarnation. But great though these differences are, they must not blind us to the fact that magico-religious beliefs, wherever found and however practised, always serve the same basic psychological purpose, just as they invariably reflect the local cultural organization.

As in all human institutions, they show a gradation which prohibits drawing rigid boundary lines to make neat, mutually exclusive categories. Despite this a distinction is often made between two types of religious practitioner: the *shaman* and the *priest*.

The term shaman is derived from a Siberian word and it is in northern Asia that shamanism is most intensively developed. Other words having approximately the same meaning are *medicine man* (usually among Amerindians), *witch doctor* (in Africa and Melanesia) and the Eskimo *angakok*.

Shamans, who may be either men or women, are magicians of various kinds and are usually part-time practitioners. They almost always work on their own at the request of individuals or small groups of people and they usually specialize in exorcizing or cajoling evil spirits. They also provide charms to avert bad luck, diagnose and cure illness, interpret dreams, and sometimes practise sorcery. It is common for their seances to last for several hours, during which time they work themselves up into a state of hysterical trance, often with the help of hallucinogenic fungi or other plants. They may be out of control and need physical restraint during the session. They partly hypnotize their audience by a wide range of devices: long hours of monotonous drum beats, fumes from braziers, remarkable feats of ventriloquism so that the spectators cannot tell whose voice is speaking or where it comes from, vibrations of the tent, apparently supernatural movement of surrounding objects and much else. A great deal of this is clever conjuring and deliberate trickery. But shamans are undoubtedly convinced of their own powers and many genuinely believe that spirits are acting through them. They are usually mentally unbalanced, sometimes subnormal, often schizophrenic. Their good fortune is to live in societies where psychological aberrations of this kind are canalized into socially approved ways. With us such persons are confined in mental hospitals. Great power and prestige is the reward of a successful shaman or angakok.

Priests differ from shamans in many ways. They are more likely to be concerned with public ceremonies for the general benefit of the village, tribe or nation. They are much more commonly men than women. They are far less likely to be mentally unbalanced and are hardly ever subnormal. The reason for this is that instead of functioning on their own they are usually associated with others in an organized priesthood. Such a priesthood needs to exclude the presence of disrupting personalities. It is also the storehouse of a highly sophisticated body of learning. In some cases, as among the Zuni pueblo dwellers of New Mexico, only men of high intelligence could learn the hours-long prayers and ritual that are necessary.

Priests are more often full-time practitioners than are shamans. They are not necessarily thought of as being imbued with any divinity or possession by a god. They may simply be mediators between the earthly and the divine. Through their knowledge of the proper formulae and rituals they can intercede with the high gods on behalf of their congregations. They are the guardians of the theology and mythology of their religion but their work also spills over into the secular when they control education and artistic productions.

In ancient Rome the ordinary workman, small farmer or humble shopkeeper was probably reluctant to ask favours direct from Jupiter. The father of the gods was too terrible, too unpredictable. In a good mood he might grant a petition; in a bad mood he might hurl a thunderbolt or reduce a man to sickness and bondage. The common people of Rome felt more at ease with their *lares* and *penates*, with the humble divinities of limited power but also of limited wrath. Rather than badger Jupiter, Minerva or Mars with

ill-timed requests there was an army of little gods and goddesses
to whom one could turn at every moment of life. There was
Vagitanus to bring forth the baby's first cry, Cuba to guard it in
its crib, Educa to teach it to suckle, Fabulinus coaxed out its first
words and Domiduca turned its wandering steps safely home-
ward. All through life homely gods of this sort were to hand. If
for great occasions, for the welfare of the nation, Jupiter had to
be invoked, it was the awful and delicate task of the professional
priesthood to offer up the necessary sacrifices and prayers.

Where a priesthood is found it is likely to be in a society with
a sufficiently rich economy to support a fairly large population.
Two basic types occur: (a) priesthoods, such as the ancient Roman
one, which are chiefly concerned to maintain the cult of one or
several deities; and (b) those in which heads of families, in ancestor worshipping societies, serve as priestly mediators between
a kinship group and its dead ancestors.

But, as with magic and religion, priests and shamans substan-
tially overlap in practice. One man will frequently act in a dual or
ambivalent role (Plate x).

It was said above that priests are often concerned with *mythology*. This plays an important part in the imaginative life of most
peoples because it provides a justification of the existing social
order. It usually consists of a large number of stories, poems and
legends accounting for the origin of the world, the people in it, the
various events they experience or the peculiar features of their
culture. In many peoples these mythological accounts are very
contradictory. Where there is an organized priesthood one of its
functions may be to eliminate these inconsistencies.

Creation myths are almost universal. A curious feature is that
very often the supremely powerful gods who brought the world
into being, 'Nyame of the Ashanti, for instance, are not much
worshipped nor believed to be greatly concerned with everyday
affairs.

Many myths relate how plants or animals came by their present
appearance, especially those which are valuable food sources or
have other strong cultural associations. A legend of the Creek
Indians of Alabama tells that the animals, headed by Nokosi the
Bear, met to decide how to divide day and night. Some wanted day
to last all the time, others wanted nothing but night. Chew-
thlock-chew, the ground squirrel, said, 'Let us divide them

equally like the light and dark rings in the tail of Wotko the Racoon.' This was agreed and Nokosi, in envy, scratched Chew-thlock-chew's back. That is why ground squirrels now have stripes there.

In primitive societies, where kinship ties are felt to be emotionally close over a wide group of relatives, illness and death may be even more disrupting than with us. So we find that myths to explain the origin of death are common. A typical one is the Zulu legend of the creator god Unkulunkulu who sent a chameleon with a message to mankind saying 'Never die'. But the chameleon was slow and Unkulunkulu changed his mind and sent a lizard instead saying 'Let men die'. The chameleon arrived at last, but too late. The lizard had got there first and the fate of mankind was sealed.

Some myths symbolize wish-fulfilments that result from the insecurity of a harsh environment. The Arunta of the Central Australian desert believe in a supreme deity, Aljira, who lives in the heavens. There, the Milky Way is a great river which never runs dry. Beside it plants and fruits are plentiful and vast hunting grounds abound with tasty wallabies, birds, lizards and every sort of game. Like the aborigines, of course, Aljira is polygynous and his many beautiful wives gather herbs and berries for him. The stars are his camp fires.

Where totemism exists, myths are commonly found to explain its origin. One of these from Tikopia describes how once upon a time a foreign god called Tikarau came to a Tikopian feast but by a trick stole all the food and ran off with it. The ancestor gods of Tikopia chased him and when he fell (a deep hollow in a hillside marks the spot!) one seized a yam, another a taro, another a breadfruit and the fourth a coconut. Thus they rescued their chief foodstuffs for posterity and these are today, in that order, the totems of the Kafika, Taumako, Fangarere and Tafua clans.

Kinship behaviour and other social observances find their validation in mythology. A Nyakyusa myth tells how a chief once saw his son's beautiful wife asleep and fell in love with her. This so shocked the people that they decreed that henceforth a father-in-law and a daughter-in-law should never again look at each other – which is the rule still observed.

These examples are enough to show that mythology is something far more than a collection of ancient legends or 'just so'

stories. It is a vital part of the cultural heritage and its real importance is that it symbolically expresses social values. It justifies
present practice in terms of past events.

We have seen that magic is greatly concerned to bring about
some positive result: to make rain fall, crops grow, game abound
or enemies die. But it has its negative aspect – the averting of evil
or witchcraft. To do this, elaborate spells may be recited (Fig. 39)
or complicated rituals performed. Often all that is needed is to
carry a simple talisman or lucky charm. In our own society we are
familiar with such objects as a hare's foot, a miniature black cat,
a crucifix, swastika or horseshoe (Fig. 40). However common these
may be, their adoption is usually left to individual taste and caprice.

In many societies we meet a form of negative magic which is
binding on the entire community or at least on large sections of it.
This is what is called a *taboo*. It is a rule which forbids people to
do something; to disregard it brings automatic punishment by

39 The Tibetan prayer 'Om mani padme hum' written in different
scripts. (After Forstmann.)

40 Lucky 'charms'. Left to right: Swastika; the Egyptian *ankh* hieroglyph; the pentacle; crucifix; horseshoe.

supernatural means. Almost any act or kind of behaviour can be
tabooed and the result of infringement may be loss of power,
property or status, illness or even death. Taboos always reflect
other elements of the culture, more especially those which are
prominent in the economy or social structure of the tribe. Incest
observances, which are taboos on certain sexual relationships, have
already been mentioned. Avoidance rules carry this principle
further, whilst among the Swazi, as elsewhere, a wife is tabooed
from using the names of her husband's senior male relatives, or
even from using syllables which resemble them in sound. In
Polynesia high-ranking chiefs are deeply imbued with *mana*.
Taboos restrict what they may do, lest their power should harm
baser mortals, who are themselves tabooed from various acts
directed against the chiefs. By this means social stratifications are
maintained, which may be reinforced by taboos forbidding commoners to eat certain types of food. Indeed, prohibitions on food
are among the commonest taboos. Clansmen are often forbidden
to eat their totem animal, in Australia almost always so. But other
eating restrictions occur. In the Kakadu tribe a boy, after one of
the initiation ceremonies, must avoid many foods including certain
kinds of yams, lizards, snakes, flying foxes, emu, female opossums
and turtles. This taboo, as well as having its magico-religious
implications, reflects the economy of a society which depends on
an uncertain food supply and the political organization in which
youths are much less privileged than older men. In Hawaii it was
taboo for women to eat bananas or coconuts, or for men and
women to eat together. This emphasized the different status and
roles of the sexes – a widespread function of the custom.

A special form of Polynesian taboo is known as *rahui*. This was
a prohibition against trespassing on lands or fishing sites owned by
chiefs and nobles. It is another example which reflects the basic

economy and social structure. *Noa* is a term used to describe the cancelling of a taboo, as when food which was forbidden to everyone during its growing stages was released for general consumption after the first fruits had been offered to the gods.

Several examples of the organization of culture have been given and more can be inferred from details referred to in this book. Culture and society may be compared with machinery. A car, for instance, will have a battery, a carburettor, a distributor, plugs, a gasket, cylinders, a fan-belt and many other parts. Each is interesting but none, isolated from the whole motor, can be understood in a functional sense. Equally, the innumerable separate elements which make up the culture of any society can be understood only when their interrelationships are established. Until then the society cannot be comprehended as a functioning unity. But once this has been achieved the anthropologist can only be left with a profound respect for the efficiency with which these primitive communities have evolved their social orders.

Many further examples of the integration of different aspects of culture might be given. Even manifestations of mental disease – the abnormal – are closely geared to the behaviour patterns which are normal to a society.

When primitive communities are exposed to white infiltration and to the economic, social, religious and other pressures which always accompany it, deep feelings of insecurity and resentment are aroused (with good reason) in the natives. Their pattern of life is profoundly modified. In many groups personal readjustment may be impossible, in view of the rigidity of tribal organization. When this happens one of the commonest responses has been the development of some kind of religious revival among the primitives. In Oceania these episodes are known as *cargo cults* because a typical feature of them is the belief that the ancestor gods will return on a ship laden with *mana* in various forms. The white men will then be driven away and the old tribal order restored. In North America similar cults have developed. As a result of the disruption of Indian traditional life under increasing white domination, a universal feeling of hopelessness oppresses them. A native prophet is then likely to arise and promise that the ancestral dead will come again and sweep the white man from the land, restore the buffalo and deer, and re-establish the old customs and traditional values. All that is needed is faith and the performance of a few dances or other rituals. In 1869 a Paiute Indian of Nevada began to preach a cult of this kind, which is known as the 'First Ghost Dance'. It spread rapidly west of the Rockies and by 1871 the tribes of California were in a ferment. Even more famous is the Second Ghost Dance of 1890, which spread hysterically among the Dakota, Arapaho, Kiowa and other Plains tribes. It was started by a medicine man named Wovoka and his dances were of the usual kind, embracing visions, fits and frenzy. Many religious upheavals of this sort have been recorded elsewhere in the Americas and also in South Africa, Nigeria and New Guinea.

Here, for lack of space, we must leave this brief review. However important magico-religious activities may be, there are very few societies which are obsessed by them. Most people in most communities go about their daily affairs much as we do. They work, win food from the environment, play, make love, sleep and dream. If, on the whole, they are rather more occupied with the supernatural than we are, this merely reflects the fact that they are still ignorant of a few scientific facts which we now know. A very short step into the past takes us to an England, or New England, aflame with superstition, where any house could harbour a witch, any bed conceal an incubus, and any man's chapel (except one's own) be a coven of devils. It has been said that the history of scientific progress lies less in the discovery of great truths than in our gradual emancipation from error. Primitive peoples differ from us only in being, so far, slightly less emancipated.

9 LAW

How men live in harmony

Law, customs, mores, offences, motives, legal
procedure, clan vengeance, collective responsibility, Plains Indians, African law, *lex talionis*,
oaths, ordeals, social conformity.

An anthropologist is likely to be greatly interested in the legal
system of any peoples, primitive or advanced, whom he is study-
ing. All societies have some pattern of behaviour to which the
term *law* can be applied but its definition is very difficult. In everyday speech the word is used in many senses, as a glance at *The
Concise Oxford Dictionary* will show. Two common uses may be
illustrated. When we say: 'The law in England often moves
slowly but it tries to be impartial', the word law refers to procedures
which take place in courts; to the opinions, decisions and pro-
nouncements of various kinds of judges and magistrates; to the
processes of litigation which enable society to punish criminals or
permit civil litigants to settle disputes. In this sense law is dynamic.
It is a system of behaviour; a patterned form of social activity. If,
however, we say: 'The law of England makes murder a felony',
the word law has a more static meaning. It refers to that collection
of rules based on the authority of parliament or which have evolved
down the centuries and are now recognized as binding on individuals to such an extent that their breach may lead to the imposition
of some penalty by a court of justice.

This definition is incomplete, but certain points about it should
be noted. The 'rules' referred to are, of course, rules of conduct or
behaviour but they are not the same as *customs*. It is a custom in
England for men's coats to be buttoned left side over right, women's
right over left. But if someone buttons a coat in the reverse way
he incurs no legal penalty. Nor are laws the same as *mores*. Mores
(singular *mos*) are customs about which people have a very strong
emotional feeling. (The word *moral* comes from the same Latin
root.) Their breach stirs up rage, ill-feeling or disgust but only
sometimes will it also be a violation of the law.

With us breaking the law may incite strong feelings in the
community, as when a man cruelly flogs a defenceless girl. Or it

may evoke little notice, or even sympathy for the offender, as happens when someone commits a minor traffic offence, takes a last drink in a pub 'after time' or buys a lottery ticket in the wrong way. Sympathy with people who have broken the law is very common in Western societies when the laws they break are themselves unpopular. The law enforcing prohibition in the U.S.A. was much resented and millions of people were in full sympathy with anyone who defied it. It remained the law for several years, however, and during that time it was as far as possible enforced by the *state*.

This gives us another view of it. If we ask: 'What is the state?' we find that one answer is to define it as that association of people which successfully claims the monopoly of *legitimate physical force*. State and law in this view are two aspects of the same thing.

In primitive societies the situation is different. There is no parliament to devise complicated regulations which please some sections of the tribe whilst annoying others. Preliterate man is seldom torn between multiple standards. So some anthropologists describe law simply as the rules enforced by the overwhelming body of public opinion. It is what almost the entire group thinks is the proper way for a man to behave towards his neighbours. Seen like this, law is hardly to be distinguished from customs and mores. It is not, as with us, something that is written in statute books or laid down by precedent in the courts. It is the traditional wisdom and decisions of the community. If any part of it is felt to be intolerable or irksome it is modified by common consent: but modified spontaneously rather than deliberately. This again is an incomplete definition. It would be too simple to apply in many of the Bantu African societies. But we need to be less concerned to define law than to consider some of its attributes and how it functions as a part of every culture.

Broadly speaking, it can be said that law is one of the mechanisms serving to regulate relationships between members of a society. By asserting what is permitted or forbidden it eases the integration of individuals or groups. It aims to prevent conduct likely to disrupt social cohesion and tries to dispose of trouble, as quickly as possible, in order to restore harmony.

Under primitive conditions we find that the types of offences which people can commit are different and far fewer than with us. For example, at a really primitive level theft may be almost impossible since no one has anything to steal except a few clothes, weapons and tools which would be instantly recognized if the thief tried to use them. The theft of food may be an exception and it can be a serious offence in tribes that are near the starvation level. But it will often never arise owing to the strong patterns of mutual sharing among primitive groups or because it shames a man by revealing his inability to hunt, fish or grow enough yams to support his family.

In advanced societies offences are basically of two kinds. *Crimes*, which are normally dealt with by a state prosecution as being offences against the community, and *torts*, which are dealt with by civil actions in which one person sues another for purely personal reasons. The first includes, with us, murder, bigamy, arson, fraud and serious assaults; the second covers such offences as slander, trespass, breach of contract and some forms of negligence. We must be careful not to transpose too precisely our own legal concepts into the very different systems which are found among tribal groups. Rough equivalents of crimes and torts do exist, however, as judged by the method of retaliation – whether public or private.

In many primitive societies, such as the Eskimo or Dobuans, even murder is not a crime because no attempt is made by the community to punish the murderer. It remains, as we would say, a tort – a purely personal offence that may be avenged privately by the victim's relatives but calls for no general action against the killer. In contrast to this, breach of a taboo is often a most serious crime because it is felt that it may stir up magical forces that will endanger everyone in the tribe. Adultery may be a grave offence because it disrupts family and clan groups, but there is no general rule about this. Its significance depends on the relationship of the offending parties, the social structure and much else. Witchcraft, too, is commonly thought to be a grossly antisocial offence. Among most of the Amerindians of the Great Plains, such as the Blackfoot, Hidatsa, Dakota, Pawnee, Mandan and Omaha, it was a crime for a man to hunt buffalo before the tribal council had decided that the right time had come. This was because a solitary hunter might scare the herds away and leave the rest of the tribe short of food. In fact, the chief function of the *akicita* or tribal police in the Plains Indians seems to have been this prevention of unofficial buffalo hunting. But it is also a curious fact, and one which is difficult to explain, that among the Comanche and the Sarsi, two of the most typical of the Plains tribes, the police seem not to have exercised this function.

A striking difference between primitive and advanced communities is reflected in our dictum that 'ignorance of the law is no excuse for breaking it'. This arises from the fact that with us ignorance of the law is very common. There are many thousands of laws and by-laws and no one, not even a professional lawyer, can know them all. Among such people as the Yaghan of Tierra del Fuego or the Tupinamba of Brazil a person is hardly ever in doubt. Apart from the rare occasion when someone is completely insensitive to tribal opinion, an individual always knows how the community will expect him to act in any situation.

In Western society our intentions, when we break the law, do not excuse our crime or misdemeanour but they may greatly alter the seriousness with which it is viewed. If we fatally shoot a man with the deliberate intention of killing him, that is murder. If we intend to shoot only near enough to scare him but by some unlucky chance the bullet kills him, that would probably be manslaughter. If we killed him by accident and entirely without negligence on our part, that would not be a crime.

In many primitive societies the offence is judged solely on the basis of its effect. The motive or other circumstances are then ignored. What matters is the result of a man's action. If an injury has been done or a loss inflicted, retribution must be made or compensation awarded. This may be paid to the victim, his family, clan or, as among the Zulu, to his chief. Even in quite advanced societies, such as the great African nations which are distinguished for the complexity of their legal systems and for the elaborate proceedings in their courts of law, there is often little attention given to motive nor, indeed, was there in Anglo-Saxon England, as emerges very clearly from the law codes of King Aethelberht of Kent and King Alfred of Wessex. But some African groups recognize provocation as an extenuating circumstance; the Yurok of California demanded a higher rate of injury compensation when malice aforethought could be proved, and the Ifugao, a primitive rice-growing people of the Philippine Islands, claim no compensation for even serious injuries if accidentally inflicted. This is also found in some Bantu groups.

The actual way in which legal problems are dealt with varies

greatly from one primitive group to another (Plate XII). In stratified
societies there is usually a hierarchical system whereby heads of
families, village headmen, district or paramount chiefs decide legal
issues and pronounce judgements at progressively higher levels.
They may or may not be assisted by courts of various kinds.
    In segmented societies small local and kinship groups function
as autonomous units. The commonest are clans, offences between
which are often dealt with by *clan vengeance*. This means that all
members of a clan will unite to support a clansman injured by
anyone from another clan and will retaliate or demand compensation for the injury. If the wrongdoer cannot give satisfaction, all
his clansmen may be held liable for his offence. This is the principle of collective responsibility, which is another expression of
the close identification of an individual with his group. It may
also apply to lineage, village or other social groupings. During
World War II the Nazis forced it on Jews. Clans usually unite in
support of their members irrespective of the rights or wrongs at
issue. But if a man offends too often he may be rejected by his
group because, as a persistent trouble-maker, he is felt to be more
of a liability than an asset. In Eskimo villages a man usually gets
away with one murder without public intervention. If he makes a
habit of the offence the community will combine to kill him
because Eskimo who start too many blood feuds upset the delicate
social equilibrium of these tiny groups and probably throw too
great a strain on the economy by reducing the number of hunters
to a level which is dangerous for the village as a whole. Legal
activity of this kind is only just above the level of complete
informality.
    In general, the American Plains Indians are distinguished by
their intensely individualistic pattern of culture. This is shown in
their rough and ready justice, which is largely of the retaliatory
kind based on tit-for-tat settlement between aggrieved persons.
This adds interest to the occasions when they combine to form
small disciplinary bodies for special purposes. We have already
referred to one of the commonest of these, the Police Societies. As
well as regulating the buffalo hunt, they kept order when a tribe
was on the move, acted as scouts and guards, rounded up strag-
glers, restrained the impetuous and served as keepers of the public
peace at the sacred Sun Dance and other tribal gatherings. As far
as possible these police kept control by persuasion rather than

force. But as a last resort or for serious offences they had power to punish. The usual punishment was whipping, with or without destruction of the culprit's tipi, bows, horses or other property. Of outstanding interest is the fact that the purpose of punishment was to reform the wrongdoer, not revenge. In the Assiniboine and Plains-Ojibway, for example, if a man promised to mend his ways after he had been punished he was at once presented with presents of horses or blankets and reinstated into a new position in the tribe. This aim of legal action, so as to produce social conformity and reintegration on the part of the transgressor, contrasts with what is found in many groups. Often it is the law abiding persons who are stimulated to continued conformity by the spectacle of the dire penalties inflicted on law breakers.

Plains police action reflects the values that were important for the survival of the society: economic security from the hunt, proper relationships with the supernatural powers, the regulation of affairs between tribes and the preservation of unity within groups where disruptive bickering was a dangerous luxury. Although the system was a simple one its organization and social approval leave no doubt about its full legal status.

In peoples such as the Eskimo, the Siberian Chuckchi, the Omaha and the Ona of Tierra del Fuego there is virtually nothing which corresponds to our concept of a trial to establish a person's innocence or guilt. Usually everyone knows that the culprit has committed a crime: the legal system merely organizes punishment or decides what compensation shall be made. Early travellers and anthropologists noted the absence of an over-arching state organization in segmented societies such as these and were at a loss to explain the evident cohesion and sense of 'oneness' which their members felt. They had expected to find a condition of anarchy with each man's hand ever raised against his fellows. The lack of such bloody chaos added support to the concept of 'the noble savage' – of virtuous and peaceful aboriginal man, automatically law-abiding from primeval instinct. This theory failed under closer scrutiny but the general puzzle of primitive social cohesion remained. In an Australian horde, of a few hundred persons, family ties might have accounted for the absence of 'anarchy'. But the Nuer of the Sudan are also a segmented society with a population around a quarter of a million. Yet despite the fact that their tribes, clans and lineages are not united by any overruling political power they, too, show no sign of anarchy. We now realize that the bonds which unite people into a functioning society are to be found in their social structure: in the interrelationship of their kinship organization, clan system and local grouping. The pattern of their legal system is also extremely important. Social cohesion was greatly strengthened among the Yurok of California by an elaborate juridical organization which nevertheless functioned in the total absence of any public officials to put the code into effect. The 100,000 Ifugao are another segmented society who are highly litigious. Lacking a centralized political power, their customary law makes obligations and penalties explicit for everyone to know. Their complicated legal code is a major contribution to stability in this society of bilateral kin groups.

In many African societies, such as the Ashanti and the Bemba, a much more elaborate legal system is found with full-scale trials. Great variety of detail is found but the Jagga of Mount Kilimanjaro may be taken as fairly typical. Trials are held in public. Village and district headmen try certain offences which on appeal go to the chief, who is also supreme judge. Other offences are tried by his court alone. The plaintive and the defendant give evidence and witnesses are heard for both sides. An experienced functionary, chosen for his eloquence, legal knowledge and astuteness, attends to represent clan interests. Another man of high standing brings religious solemnity to the occasion by performing sacrifices and divination before the trial opens. Legal fees are payable to various officials at different stages of the trial, usually in the form of cattle or goats, which, of course, reflect the value judgements of the community. The chief, or his senior advisors, may keep an eye on proceedings in lower courts and will intervene if a miscarriage of justice seems imminent. Or he may interfere if he favours one of the parties. At the end of the trial an official verdict is given and powers to enforce the judgement are available. As well as considering the verbal evidence of the plaintiff, defendant and witnesses, the court may have relied on two other forms of evidence to determine the verdict. These are the *oath* and the *ordeal*. Among peoples who are much concerned with supernatural forces an oath, sworn on a sacred object, is something of compelling power. Probably few guilty persons can swear they are innocent without revealing themselves as perjurors. This is because the form of the oath invokes upon a liar terrible retribution of a supernatural kind. The ordeal is a widespread kind of torture in which the results are believed to disclose the truth automatically. The Jagga are one of many African groups who use it. They may force the accused man to swallow a drink poisoned with datura, which has been prepared by the tribal witch doctor. If the victim vomits he will recover and is therefore innocent, if he dies he must have been guilty. In another form he is made to hold a piece of hot iron; if it burns him he is guilty. Ordeal, though common in Africa, is rare in the New World. Fines, beating or mutilation are common sentences in African courts and, formerly, some tribes had a wide repertoire of offences for which the penalty was death. When a man has been found guilty of injuring someone, a few societies take elaborate care to make the punishment fit the crime by resembling it as closely as possible. This is the principle that is found in the Exodus book of the Old Testament, where it is expressed as 'eye for eye, tooth for tooth, hand for hand, foot for foot, burning for burning, wound for wound, stripe for stripe'. It is called the *lex talionis*. Among the Jagga this kind of penalty was carried out with pedantic attention to detail but they are not typical of most African groups in this respect.

It is probably correct to say that justice is achieved in African trials far more often than it miscarries. But bad verdicts do occur. In groups with this type of social structure – that is, in stratified societies – the hierarchy of king, chiefs, headmen, commoners and slaves opens the way for abuses. Powerful rulers often behave with arbitrary injustice and inflict punishments that are despotic and cruel. A chief may kill a man on some trivial charge merely to gain possession of his wife; he may banish him in order to grab his cattle or his crops. In general, however, public opinion is likely to curb excessive tyranny. If a native king carries it too far he may be killed or deposed.

Litigation among many of these African societies is especially concerned with such offences as non-payment of lobola or other breaches of marriage contracts; with disputes about land tenure, irrigation rights, trespass, theft, goods and services; with actions for slander, adultery, murder and lesser assaults; incest; defiance of the chief or tribal council; and witchcraft or sorcery.

It is clear that legal systems of this complexity do not exist in a cultural vacuum. They ramify into every facet of tribal life. They reflect economic interests; social structure in terms of class, clan and kin; magico-religious beliefs and much else. In other words, Bantu law, as in all other societies, is completely functional as far as the total cultural organization is concerned.

After this brief discussion of the sorts of offences which may be committed, and the trial and punishment of culprits who break the law, there remains one most important question to ask: Why do most persons, most of the time, in most societies obey the law and not transgress it? To answer this adequately would need a long chapter. Social conformity is achieved in many ways. Perhaps the strongest inducement is the pressure of public opinion, which includes kinsfolk, clansmen, village neighbours and all other persons whose goodwill is sought or whose censure is feared. Many societies accord high prestige to the law-abiding man, a prestige which reaps rewards in enhancement of status, political power, wealth or *mana* – but which is often an end in itself. Failure to conform leads to public contempt or even ostracism, a sentence little better than death to many primitives. It must be realized, too, that in some societies, the Ashanti for instance, crimes are also sins because they offend the ancestral spirits or other supernatural beings. Similarly taboos are powerful negative sanctions which compel observance in hundreds of tribes by virtue of their inherent magic and awful power.

10 LANGUAGE

The gift of tongues

Origin, linguistic families, phonetic change,
phonemes, morphemes, language and culture,
social structure, tabooed words, glottochronology, language and prehistory, writing, pictograms, ideograms, phonetic scripts.

There is nothing in which man is so different from the apes as in
his power of speech – not even in his ability to make things.

To talk is an essential characteristic of the human race and to
lack speech is to be sub-human.

We cannot, then, ignore the subject of language and because of
its importance we must discuss it in some detail.

Early Palaeolithic men had to hunt, they used fire, they made
stone – and no doubt wooden – tools of varying complexity; later,
they painted on cave walls and some of them left traces which
indicate belief in an after life. Cultures of this richness could
hardly be transmitted from one generation to another, without
language, merely by young people imitating their elders. In
remote prehistoric times life was shorter than it is today. Probably
most people, even if they had survived to adult life, were dead
before they were thirty-five. At that age their children must still
have been very young, so the period of contact between one
generation and the next was brief. In these circumstances language
must have been the most important means of teaching the accumulated knowledge of previous generations. It would have had high
survival value.

Evidently speech is one of the most archaic of human activities.
It probably evolved at the same time as man himself. But how it
came about is a mystery. Some people think that the first words
must have been imitations of natural sounds (what are called
onomatopoeic words) like 'crash', 'plonk', 'murmur' or 'cuckoo'.
Others believe that they were elaborate developments of the simple
calls of animals – the grunts, howls and chatterings of our monkey
cousins. We cannot know and it is idle to guess.

Few people can speak more than half a dozen languages; most
of us speak only one . . . and only part of that one. But there may

be nearly 3,000 different languages that are spoken throughout the world, many of them by only a few scores of people, the last remnants of disappearing tribes. Now, although a man who speaks any one of these languages may know no other, they would not all be equally difficult for him to learn. Some languages he would find easy because they are closely related to his own, others might have only a moderate likeness to it and be difficult for him, whilst hundreds of others would be quite unlike anything he knew and would be very difficult indeed.

Languages which are closely related are said to belong to the same *linguistic family* or *stock*. Within these families, which vary in size just as human families do, certain members will be more closely related than others and we can then speak of *branches* of a linguistic family. A few examples will make this clear. Over much of Europe and South-West Asia we find languages that belong to the Indo-European or Aryan family.* It includes tongues as diverse as English, French, Icelandic, Classical Greek, Hindustani, Welsh and Polish, all of which share many features in common. But because these examples also have important differences we do not classify them in a single branch of the family. French belongs to the branch known as the Romance languages, which includes Italian, Spanish, and Portuguese. Icelandic belongs to the Teutonic or Germanic branch together with German, Swedish, Dutch, Yiddish and Danish (Fig. 41). Polish is a Slavic language like Russian, Czech and Croat. Whilst Hindustani, with Hindi, Bengali and Sanskrit, falls into the Indic branch.

In other parts of the world we find other linguistic families such as Semitic, which includes Hebrew, Arabic and the ancient Assyrian and Babylonian; Sinitic, with Chinese, Tibetan and Burmese; and many other families with their branches wherever men are found.

Some languages seem to be unrelated to any others: they are like solitary people who have no relatives at all. Basque is one of these. It is spoken along the western regions of the Pyrenees in France and Spain and it may be the last surviving fragment of a once widespread language spoken by prehistoric men of the Stone Age.

By 'related' languages we mean, quite simply, that they are descended from a common ancestor or source, and this relation-

* The term 'Aryan' should *never* be used to describe people or races.

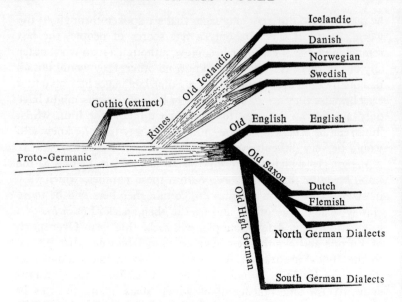

41 Diagram to illustrate the relationship of languages within the Germanic branch of the Aryan linguistic family.

ship may be recognized in any of the three main elements that go to make up a language. These are: (1) its sounds; (2) its words; (3) the way its sounds and words are arranged when people speak it – that is, its grammar and syntax. Again a few examples will make this clear.

We classify French, Italian and Spanish together because they belong to the Romance branch of the Indo-European family. They are all descended from Latin and thousands of words in each of these languages have a Latin origin. But beyond their common vocabulary they have many grammatical features in common which they have inherited from their Latin grandparent. This can be strikingly shown by the present tense of the verb *to be*:

ENGLISH	LATIN	FRENCH	SPANISH	ITALIAN
I am	sum	je suis	yo soy	io sono
thou art	es	tu es	tu eres	tu sei
he is	est	il est	él es	lei è
we are	sumus	nous sommes	nosotros somos	noi siamo
you are	estis	vous êtes	vosotros sois	vo siete
they are	sunt	ils sont	ellos son	loro sono

Notice the general pattern of resemblance within the Romance group and their Latin ancestor and how English stands clearly apart.

There are, of course, many English words which are very like or even the same as their French and Latin equivalents:

ENGLISH	FRENCH	LATIN
voice	voix	vox
infant	enfant	infans
salt	sel	sal
rose (the flower)	rose	rosa
tavern	taverne	taberna
cucumber	concombre	cucumis

This is usually because they were brought in by French-speaking Normans after the Conquest. The English relationship with German is seen in such a word as *stone*, which is *stein* in modern German, both having diverged from Old Germanic *stane*.

Sometimes when words descend from an earlier to a later language they remain unaltered, but usually they change in the process. There must once have been a word meaning 'foot' in the (now lost) parent Indo-European language from which Greek, Latin, German and English are ultimately derived. Whatever the word may have been it changed as it came into the daughter languages. So we have: Greek πους (Genitive ποδος), Latin *pes* (*pedis*), German *fuss* and English *foot*. The sound shifts in this group of words are not haphazard. They occur regularly in many others and in other Aryan languages. They illustrate what is meant by a *law of phonetic change* – in this case the famous Grimm's law, which was the first to be discovered.

Many phonetic laws have now been worked out and they show that in passing from one language to another the sounds of which words are made change in a more or less constant manner according to the languages involved.

These separate sounds, which we recognize as essential to make any word, are called *phonemes*. They are the basic elements of every word we use.

The human mouth can make an astonishing variety of sounds and if we were to add up all the phonemes used in all languages there would be many hundreds of them. They would include scores of different vowel sounds (some of which we meet no further afield than French); many consonants which would be unfamiliar to our ears; the use of different 'tones' to change the meaning of words, as in the Chinese or the African Bantu languages; the 'clicks' of the Khoisan dialects used by Hottentots; 'implosive' *b* sounds; strange gutturals; glottal stops; and a complicated series of whistling noises in Mazateco, a central American language.

Although all these sounds are available for making words, no single language ever uses more than a few dozen: between forty and fifty is about the average. Some languages use only half that number. In Lepu' Tau, a language of Borneo, there are only twenty-four phonemes.

The capacity of a language to express ideas does not depend, however, on the number of phonemes it uses. More important is the number of *morphemes* available.

Morphemes are rather like building bricks of different shapes and sizes that can be put together to construct houses of varied designs (Fig. 42). They are what we may call the 'idea units' in any language. For example, in English the sound -*s* at the end of a word often serves as a morpheme giving the idea of 'more than one', as when we add it to the singular '*dog*' to make the plural '*dogs*'. Another morpheme that sometimes expresses the same idea is -*en*, as in *oxen* or in the dialect plurals *house–housen*; *mouse–mesen*. In verbs the morpheme -*ing* usually gives the idea of action that still goes on, -*ed* suggests action that is now past. So we find *I am walking, they are eating* where the action is still continu*ing*, as opposed to *he walked, you shouted* where the action is now finish*ed*.

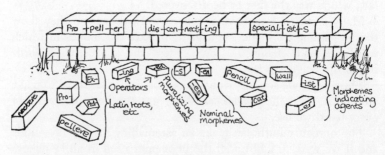

42 Diagram to represent the way in which morphemes are used to build words and sentences.

The prefixes *ab-*, *anti-*, *pre-* are morphemes (from Latin originals) conveying ideas of *away from*, *against* and *before*. 'Idea units' of this kind are much used to build up proprietary names in advertising: *Polyfilla* (a plaster suitable for filling many crevices), *Sellotape* (a plastic ribbon for sealing envelopes, etc.), *Brylcreme* (a shiny hair dressing), *Sanatogen* (a drink intended to promote health) are a few examples. Sometimes whole words are fused to produce a modification of the idea represented by each alone, as *railroad*, *pintable* and *overdraft*.

Provided morphemes are available as building bricks a language can always form new words to describe fresh ideas, new discoveries and inventions, or importations from other cultures. And it is interesting that, no matter how restricted the language of a primitive tribe may be, it seems as though *all* languages have, in fact, an unlimited capacity to expand and to meet any demands that are made on them.

We have just spoken of 'the language of a primitive tribe' but this is not the same as a primitive language. No tongue is more primitive than another. All languages have their roots weaving back into the mists of time, back to the beginning of human speech. All have an equally long ancestry, though some (such as English) have had their present form for a much shorter time than others (such as Greek). The duration of a language has no bearing on 'primitiveness'. A language is not primitive simply because the people who speak it have a primitive culture. The Australian aborigines have a material culture which is as primitive as any in the world. Other aspects of their culture are very complicated – their kinship systems, for example. And there is no doubt that their languages, too, are highly evolved. We have already seen how the culture of the Eskimo is starkly bare on the material side. Even so their language is a very rich one.

All European languages, and many others, need such words as *atomic fission*, *antibiotic*, *bathysphere* and thousands more to describe the complicated objects and ideas of our scientific culture. It would be unreasonable to look for their equivalents among the Boro of the Brazilian jungle or the primitive Eskimo, who know nothing of the subjects the words describe. Apart from the marginal *'sleet'* we have only one word for *snow*. In Eskimo, by contrast, there is *aput*, for snow on the ground, *qana*, falling snow, *piqsirpoq*, drifting snow, *qimuqsuq*, a snow drift and many more

K

which define variations in its texture, distribution, consistency and so on. In other words, Eskimo has developed precisely the vocabulary that meets its cultural needs as efficiently as English has done for its quite different requirements. All languages do the same. In Bedawin Arabic there is an elaborate vocabulary concerned with their essential animal the camel; Trobriand has many words to describe all aspects of yam cultivation.

Languages, therefore, are shaped by the culture of the people who speak them, and when the culture changes they change, too, to keep in step with it.

Linguistic change and acculturation, as a dynamic process, is brought about in three main ways. (1) A language may take words directly from another with which its speakers have contact: *curry, bantam, zebra, coffee, carnival, divan* and *cotton* entered English in this way. (2) It may coin new expressions: *elk-dog* was invented by American Indians to describe the horse when they first met it. (3) It may extend the meaning of existing words: Western Apache, an Athapaskan tongue of Arizona, drew on its existing anatomical vocabulary to describe parts of cars. A few of these many extensions are:

APACHE	ANATOMICAL MEANING	CAR MEANING
gən	hand + arm	frontwheels, tyres
dɔ	chin + jaw	front bumper
inda	eyes	headlights
tsɔs	veins	electrical wiring
ɛbiyi'	entrails, bowels	all machinery under the bonnet
pil	stomach	petrol tank
ji	heart	distributor
zik	liver	battery
kɛ'	foot	rear wheel

This shows culture shaping language. The reverse also occurs: language shapes culture in the sense that it influences how we think about the world and categorize what is in it.

For example, English normally makes a clear distinction between the words *wife* and *woman*. The thoughts, emotions and behaviour associated with one of the words differ from those associated with the other, despite some overlap between them. In

French *wife* and *woman* are not usually made linguistically distinct (although they can be). *Femme* normally includes both, with the result that the average Frenchman's attitude to females is somewhat different from the Englishman's. English distinguishes clearly between *host* and *guest*, not only as words but also as to the attitudes and behaviour of the people they represent. Conduct suitable in a host, such as deciding what food is to be served at meals or what wine to decant, may be quite improper in a guest and vice versa. In Greek the single word ξένος covers both *host* and *guest* but this does not imply that ancient Greeks were unable to distinguish between them. It is rather that Greek culture and Greek behaviour stressed the reciprocal and uniting aspects of the host-guest relationship, in contrast to English culture which emphasizes the differentiating aspects.

As we move further afield among the languages of the world we find many such differences in ways of thinking or what are sometimes called 'categories of thought'.

Bantu languages tend to ignore statements of time in their verbs; that is, they often lack the clear-cut past, present and future tenses of the Indo-European family. Instead, they use verbs to show different ways in which the action described by them occurs: its completeness or otherwise, its emphasis, its continuity and even the reason for it, but seldom its time. In societies which distinguish between the father's brother and the mother's brother in terms of their kinship position our word *uncle* cannot possibly be translated by a term common to both. In Mende, a Sudanese language, and in some Melanesian tongues tense is not chiefly shown by the verb but by the personal pronoun used with it. It is as though the expressions *I picked a flower, I am picking a flower* and *I shall pick a flower* were rendered *The-I-that-is-past pick a flower, The-I-of-now pick a flower* and *The-I-to-come pick a flower*. It sounds strange to our ears but it conveys the required ideas neatly and precisely.

In the Indo-European linguistic family we are used to words having gender. All French nouns must be masculine or feminine. Latin, German and Russian have neuter as well. Gender is rare in English and is applied only to people or animals: *actor/actress, fox/vixen*. This kind of gender is absent from many languages but other types occur. In Chippewa, a North American tongue, genders separate animate from inanimate objects. In some Dravidian languages of India gender separates subjects which have reason (and this includes deities and demons) from those which do not. Elsewhere genders are found for shape, texture, position, abstracts and much else. Wherever such patterns of speech occur they effect the way in which people view the world. In Kwakiutl, grammatical forms exist which make it clear whether an object under discussion is visible or invisible to the speaker at the time and also whether it is nearest to the speaker, the listener or to some third person. In Aztec there is no passive voice. In Japanese colours have certain features of verbs; in Klamath blue and green are not separated by different words and the Bemba have a generally restricted colour vocabulary. This does not mean that Klamath and Bemba eyes detect variations in the wavelength of light less well than we do. It simply means that their cultures are less concerned than ours with narrow colour distinctions. Hundreds of examples of this kind could be given but these are enough to show that the categories of thought peculiar to us are often very different from those which are expressed in foreign languages. It is not that linguistic patterns inescapably limit sensory perceptions and thought but rather that, with other cultural patterns, they direct perception and thinking into certain habitual channels.

It has already been hinted that language is intimately related to social patterns. Within any society and culture a language of general use normally occurs which is used by most people most of the time. But special groups within the total population may use modifications of it on certain occasions.

In Hawaii and some African groups 'royal' languages are found which are used only by members of the ruling house or high nobles closely associated with them. *Babytalk* systems are widespread. They tend to be grammatically impoverished and to contain words that are doubled or partly doubled: English *bye-byes* and *bow-wow* (in French *dodo* and *toutou*); Arabic *gallu-gallu* (bath); Comanche *tata* (food); Gilyak *ykyk* (hurt); or forms with special endings: *tummy*, *dolly*. Babytalk is of uncertain function. It is alleged to help infants by offering them easier words and sounds – but *pussy* is hardly more simple than *cat*. Moreover, in several languages adults use it extensively towards animals and it is also used in some wholly adult situations, as between lovers in Spanish and Marathi.

Another aspect of children's language can be seen in nursery

LANGUAGE 149

rhymes or their equivalents. A peculiar feature of these is that
they often have sixteen beats to a verse. The fact that this is found
in such totally unrelated languages as English, Arabic, Chinese,
Bengkalu (a Sumatran language), Yoruba, Serrano (an Amerindian tongue) and Trukese (of the Caroline Islands) suggests
that there may be a universal human tendency towards this
regularity. If so, it would be interesting to know its significance,
but at present our limited knowledge of exotic metrical systems
does not permit this. In some societies *women's languages* are
found; in others *men's languages* occur, and these may be special
forms used during the rituals of their secret societies. Teen-agers
often put a new twist on the language of their parents, sometimes
by giving old words a new sense or by devising phrases that are
likely to have brief popularity before being replaced by other
neologisms, as these coined expressions are called. Two common
forms of speech among young people are *back talk*, in which words
or syllables are reversed back to front, and *riming* languages. A
peculiar linguistic variant is the whistling form of Mazateco, a
Mexican tongue. This is used mostly by young people and anything that can be said in the ordinary spoken form can also be said
in whistles. It has the advantage of exceptional carrying power
when used out of doors, but the whistles can also be subdued to a
soft level so that young people may talk among themselves without
disturbing their elders in the same room. Women understand it
and can use it, although they seldom do so.

Linguistic usage reflects social structure in various ways. In the
North-west Amazonia region multilingualism is the rule: all
persons speak at least three or four languages. This arises from:
(1) the cultural identification of language with tribe; (2) tribal
exogamy, and (3) communal living in large longhouses. For
example, the second longhouse up the Inambú River belongs to
men of the Tuyuka tribe who all speak that language. Their wives
come, in about equal numbers, from three tribes, the Barasana,
Desano and Tukano. For general household conversation everyone speaks Tuyuka, but groups of tribeswomen, gossiping amongst
themselves, use their original natal language, which is overheard
by the children and other people who thus learn it. As people get
older, more languages are learned from visitors or as a result of
travel. Tatuyo and Paneroa are likely to be added and, eventually,
six or eight languages may be acquired. Here, then, multi-

lingualism serves to demarcate distinct exogamous social units.
The Gommu Koya of the Godavari watershed in India speak a
Dravidian language. They are segmented into five exogamous
phratries, are patrilineal and have preferential marriage for real or
classificatory cross cousins. Their kin relationships entail a range
of behaviour from the extreme respect due to a mother's brother,
the mutual reserve between mother and son, to the intimacy and
joking relationship between cross cousins. They have about forty
kinship terms. These are used in conjunction with a group of
prefixes and suffixes, the choice of which is determined by the
social relationship of speakers. Some of these are:

USAGE	PREFIX	SUFFIX
Respect	maa–	–aal, –ooru
Reserve		–ku
Informality		–o
Intimacy	naa–	–Du, –sk

In this way Koya language morphology reflects kinship structure
and the nuances of behaviour associated with it.

Unfortunately, language can mask social structure as well as
reveal it. One group of Tuareg of the Sahara formerly had matrilineal descent, though it is now essentially bilateral but with
property inheritance through the father. They are endogamous in
kinship groups and also within their three classes: nobles, vassals
and slaves. They have preferential marriage in descending order:
maternal cross cousin, maternal parallel cousin, paternal parallel
cousin, paternal cross cousin. Their kinship terminology, however, fails to reveal this behaviour and gives a quite false impression
of their social structure.

In Burundi, with a population of about 2,000,000, the normal
linguistic usage is explicitly differentiated according to caste, age
and sex so that speech behaviour closely reflects the social organization. But many other aspects of behaviour are displayed. In
certain embarrassing situations the Rundi value graceful lying and
clever evasions rather than truth, whereas in discussing subjects
of central interest such as kinship, economic affairs and especially

cattle, direct precise speech using minutely detailed vocabularies
is required. In forensic matters flamboyant rhetoric is highly
valued, in contrast to what is found among the Navajo, Zuni and,
nowadays, ourselves. To comprehend Rundi communication fully
a knowledge of gestures is needed. For instance, the action (or
phrase) 'I pull up grass for you' is a sign of subservience or
gratitude.

Japanese is a language in which the status of the speakers in a
conversation is very precisely defined although the substance and
the rest of the context may be left highly ambiguous. This again
reflects what is a major element of interest and concern in Japanese
culture.

An important way in which language functions in relationship
to culture and behaviour is seen in taboos on words.

When a word is tabooed it means that people dare not use it lest
some magically induced misfortune befalls them. In primitive
societies the name of a dead person is often tabooed. This presumably arises from a vague but deeply felt fear that to name a
person is to summon him and that the ghost of the dead man may
return to molest whoever utters his name. This is occasionally
extended to include words which contain syllables identical with
the name of the dead person. It is as though, after the death of a
Mr. Dent, we were unable to use the words *dental, indenture* or
dependent. Names of the living may also be tabooed. In certain
societies commoners are forbidden to name their tribal chief. Even
in England court protocol imposes restrictions of a kind, and it is
said that after the death of Albert, the Prince Consort, the widowed
Queen lamented that there was no one left who was permitted to
call her 'Victoria'.

Names of gods and demons may be tabooed or may only be safe
to use if the speaker takes magical precautions such as crossing his
fingers or reciting some special formula of words or adopting an
unusual tone of voice. The so-called 'clerical voice' formerly
affected by parsons when conducting a religious service perhaps
developed from notions of this sort.

Primitive peoples often taboo the use of certain words or topics
of conversation as part of the avoidance relationship between close
relatives. Food, clothing and other subjects of an intimate nature
may be unfit for discussion between a brother and sister once they
have grown up, or between a man and his mother-in-law.

These examples are enough to show some of the many ways in which language reflects social behaviour and other aspects of culture.

We have seen that all natural languages are derived from earlier ones and conversely that a language is likely to evolve into a number of daughter tongues. At first these will be very close to the parent, but as the centuries pass they drift further apart from the parent and from each other. Rates of change vary somewhat but the occurrence of this drift can be used to assess the length of time during which related languages have been diverging. The method of doing this is known as *glottochronology*. A list is compiled of a hundred or more basic words that refer to things of universal experience, words such as: head, sun, blood, bird and drink. The terms for these things are then written down in each of the languages being investigated and the percentage of them that are the same can be quickly calculated. The result gives the relative nearness of the languages to each other and to their parent tongue. From this an estimate may be made of how long ago each language split off the parent. This method has been applied to the Celtic group; to Tamil, Telugu, Kannada and Malayalam, four related Dravidian languages; to Eskimo dialects and to many others. Applied to Ajumawi and Atsugewi, two Hokan languages of California, glottochronology indicates a separation about 3,300 years ago. Support for this has been given by Carbon-14 dating and from archaeological evidence. It is always reassuring when different methods of investigation give consistent results.

Another way of inferring past events from languages is to look for traces of ancient origins and meanings in words that are now being used. The Navajo live in the hot south-west of the United States of America. They have a word, *àdè*, meaning a *gourd spoon* which also has older associations connected with *animal's horn*. Another word, *–sàs*, means *seed which lies on the ground*, but at an earlier level in the Athapaskan linguistic family it had the meaning *it lies like flakes of snow*. Yet another word refers to sleeplessness, but a different shade of meaning appears to connect it with the idea of paddling a canoe. This suggests that the modern form came into existence from some twist such as 'sleep paddles away from me'. The use of horn ladles, birch-bark canoes and the idea of corn lying like snow are not part of Navajo culture today. Their occurrence linguistically suggests that originally the Navajo language took shape far to the north of its present territory and was brought to its modern area by the migrating ancestors of the tribe.

Clues of this kind, which survive like fossils embedded in the deeper strata of a language, may reveal details about its early speakers that would not be guessed from the way its modern users live.

So far we have said nothing about ways in which a language can be permanently recorded once the sound of its spoken words has died away. There are now several ways of doing this but by far the most important is *writing*.

From far back in the Upper Palaeolithic period, near the end of the Old Stone Age, perhaps 20,000 or 30,000 years ago, symbolic cave paintings and carvings have been found. In the Mesolithic or Middle Stone Age period people of the Azilian culture painted curious designs on pebbles (Fig. 14). These designs, in the forms of bars, zig-zags, crosses and groups of dots remain a mystery which no one can yet explain. Perhaps no one ever will. They may be nothing more than decorations, but when we look at them and hold them in our hand it is easy to wonder whether they were meant to convey some sort of message. If so they must be one of the earliest ways in which a tiny fragment of language was recorded. If they conveyed no more than such simple messages as 'Beware!', 'Private – keep out', 'Fish in this pool', 'Bees' nest' they would still have served to make permanent in painted stone what otherwise would have faded with the uttered words. Two have been tentatively identified as symbolizing a man and a squatting woman respectively.

But these symbolic representations of simple ideas, if that is what they were, do not make a system of true writing, because writing implies more than the recording of single, disconnected images. It must be able to cope with a series of ideas in the form of a narrative, however brief.

The rudiments of true writing are found in *pictograms*. These are more or less realistic sketches of the events in a story. They often appear in the 'Puzzle Corner' of children's newspapers and they have been produced by primitive peoples in Ancient Egypt, Phoenicia, Crete, Central Africa, North America, Siberia and elsewhere. A series of these little pictures may represent events in a hunt or fight. In general, pictograms can show only actual events. Abstract ideas mostly have to be inferred from them.

Ideograms are a slight advance on this. They, too, are little sketches of objects but they are more often intended to be symbols of ideas connected with the object. In Egyptian hieroglyphs a

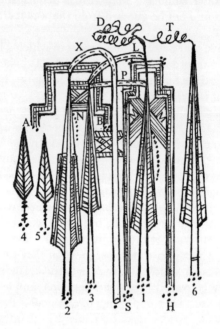

43 A love letter of a Yukaghir girl of Siberia, written on birch bark. The umbrella-shaped symbols are people. No. 1 is the Yukaghir girl (the dots at the top are her hair). She loves passionately (lines L, P) a man (No. 3) who has left her for another woman (No. 2 – whose hair is also shown by dots). No. 2 is a Russian (she has wide skirts) and lives far away (the incomplete line A–B). The Yukaghir girl is left alone in a small house (line S–H). Her passionate love (P–L) for No. 3 is thwarted by the Russian woman (line X breaks P and L). But although she and the man have had children (Nos. 4 and 5) they will nag each other and not get on together (cross hatch lines N). Though another Yukaghir man (No. 6) thinks of marrying her (T) she dreams only of her faithless lover (D). The crossed lines (MM) indicate her sorrow and misery.
The letter reads: 'You have left me alone in my home and gone far away. You live with a Russian girl and the children she has had by you but you are not happy. Despite my sorrow I love only you, although another man wants to marry me.'

common sign is the character ⌐ᵂ⌐. It is a picture of a roll of papyrus, tied and sealed and it is used to show that what is being discussed is some abstract topic. A general feature of ideograms is that they tend to convey these abstract associations of the object they depict. Writing of this kind has been found in Africa, North and Central America, Polynesia and Australia. Figure 43 is a Yukaghir example from Siberia.

Pictograms and ideograms can be read in any language. The Egyptian hieroglyph of a man with his hand to his mouth would convey the idea of eating or of hunger anywhere in the world.

The next, and by far the most important, step is the change to *phonetic script*. In this the separate characters which make up the words or images stand not for ideas but for *sounds*. As a result they are firmly related, not only to the thought which is expressed, but also to the actual words used to express it: to spoken language. They have become *phonograms*. Unlike pictograms, the shape of the signs used in phonetic writing bears no resemblance to what they represent.

Phonetic writing can be of two kinds, *syllabic* or *alphabetic*, which are sometimes combined in a single system of writing. In syllabic forms (or *syllabaries*) each of the characters that is used represents the sound of one spoken syllable of a word. Alphabetic writing goes further and represents the sounds (phonemes) that make up the syllable. For example, in Egyptian the hieroglyph

represents the sound *sa* and is therefore a syllabic sign. By itself *sa* means *son*. On the other hand ⌒ is an alphabetic sign because it stands for the single phoneme represented by our letter *t*. In Egyptian it was a feminine ending. Finally ○ is another syllabic sign, but in this case originally derived from a pictogram of the sun's disc. It has the sound value *ra* – derived from Ra the sun god and meaning either *sun* or the *god* himself according to the context. The three signs in a row would then make the word *Satra* and could be translated 'daughter of the sun' or more briefly 'sun child'. Although the word must be pronounced *Satra*, the Egyptians would write it

putting the *Ra* syllable first because it happens to be a sacred name.

The advantage of using an alphabetic script is that far fewer signs are needed to represent the number of phonemes each language uses than would be needed to represent the many syllables arising from different combinations of phonemes. All the most advanced scripts of the world are alphabetic. It was the Egyptians who first invented the device of using a single symbol to indicate separate sounds. The system spread to Semitic and Phoenician writing and, from these languages, began to change in form and to spread rapidly. Eventually all languages which came to be written used alphabets ultimately derived from these early scripts.

11 ART

Man's pursuit of beauty

The origin of art, art and culture, children in
films, who are the artists? what arts does a
society practise? the function of art.

We have already said that no one can tell when or how people
first began to speak. The origin of art is no less obscure than the
origin of language. Men could live without art as far as biological
survival is concerned but in fact they never do. In some way which
is impossible to define the practice of the arts seems as much a
hallmark of being human as the use of speech or the making of
tools. Perhaps man's capacity for being bored has something to do
with it, but this cannot be the full explanation because boredom
may be canalized into other interests such as games, trade or war.
The oldest art known to us are the paintings and sculpture left by
late palaeolithic hunters in the caves of France and Spain. To see
the beautiful bison of Altamira or the horses and reindeer at
Lascaux is to be thrilled by some of the most exciting and accomplished work that any artists have ever produced. But these works
are quite modern. The oldest of them can hardly date from much
before 30,000 B.C., which is a mere yesterday compared with the
million or more years of man's existence on earth.

This cave art has survived only because of its sheltered position.
Its advanced standard leaves no doubt that it is not the beginning
of a new activity but a skill with a long history leading up to it.
What earlier forms existed can only be surmised. Primitive peoples
today have many kinds of art: they carve wood with stone tools,
plait ornamental baskets (Figs. 44a and b), paint and tattoo their
bodies, and make elaborate designs in sand, in shells and in
feathers. All of these arts and many others would have been
possible to men of the most ancient Stone Age, the men of Java
or Chou-K'ou-Tien and even to *Homo habilis*.

But we must beware of misunderstanding when using the term
'primitive art'. Many examples are extremely complex and are a
blend of superb technical achievement with an elaborate ideology.
It is all but impossible to identify any universal feature which can
serve as a sure hallmark of primitive art. The best we can say is

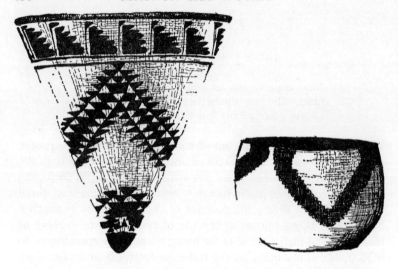

44 Maidu baskets. (*a*) The design on the rim represents mountains, on
the body flying geese; (*b*) the racoon design. (After Boas.)

that it is the art of primitive peoples and it is certain that every
known tribe has many of these skills, which are often spoken of as
the *plastic* or *graphic* arts.

There are, however, quite different arts and it may be that it
was with them that man's artistic evolution began.

Music and *dancing* are found everywhere in the world (Plate
xv). All primitive tribes have some musical instruments, though
many of these are extremely simple, as when the Yuma of Arizona
beat ordinary household baskets to make a kind of drum or the
Ipuriná coil bark to make a trumpet (Fig. 45). All peoples dance,
many in movements of great complexity (Fig. 46). Perhaps the
earliest of arts was a combination of music and dancing in which
the half-men of the pre-palaeolithic age banged bits of wood

45 Bark trumpet. Ipuriná tribe, south-west Amazonia. (After Ehren-
reich.)

46 (*Left*) Masked dancer. Bacairi tribe, Xingú River region, South America. (After Steinen.)

47 (*Right*) Mukish clown, Congo. (After Lips, and Capello and Ivens.)

together or just clapped their hands in strange rhythms whilst moving their bodies in some sort of rhythmic swing, jerk or swirl. Music and dancing are often joined with drama and pantomime. Many forms are found. Figure 47 shows one of the popular masked Mukish clowns of West Africa. They are experts at performing on stilts.

Another of the arts is that known as *oral literature*. This really means the telling of stories or the chanting of epics and legends. Again it is found among all primitive people and, like music or dancing, it is probably far more important and far more basic to their lives than the plastic and graphic arts. Often these stories are accompanied by some way of illustrating them. The string figures known as 'cats' cradles' are a widespread way of doing this (Fig. 48). They are a form of artistic expression which may demand great manual dexterity, as in many of the Eskimo examples which can be made to show moving objects or animals. Little songs, riddles, fables or 'just so' stories may have developed almost as soon as man's earliest attempts to talk. We can only guess, with scant hope of ever knowing the answer.

We can, however, be sure of one fact: the arts of any people are never an irrelevant gloss on their society and culture. They are always deeply integrated with it and express the attitudes and interests of the people who practise them. This often takes quite subtle forms as can be seen if we look at one small item out of the vast range of possible examples.

In the world of the cinema, films often handle themes dealing with the *relationship between children and adults*. If we examine a series of French, Italian, American and English films we shall find that each nationality has a typical attitude to this relationship. It is an attitude that recurs time and again but which is quite unlike that of the other countries, although all four portray the children as noble characters – usually more so than the adults around them.

French films are the least concerned with moral issues, especially with the balance between good and evil. The virtue of their children is less the result of conscious effort on the child's part than of his inevitable immaturity and incapacity for vice. These children tend to be sad and yearning; they are excluded from the world of the adults, who do not understand them. When they finally grow up and can achieve what they yearned for, they no longer want it; they find that it has 'died on them' as we say. These films teach one to master past disappointments and to resign oneself to present frustration. They emphasize the mis-timing of life: desires are not synchronized with the capacity to enjoy them, when the moment comes the zest for it has passed.

Sous les Toits de Paris, *The Male Brute* and *The Seven Deadly Sins* are French films which illustrate these points. So does *Panique*, in which the world's mis-timing is such that proof of a man's innocence of a crime comes just as he dies.

The Italian cinema is perhaps subconsciously influenced by the innumerable illustrations of the Madonna and Child which adorn churches, art galleries and people's homes. The Madonna represents the pure, unsullied woman whose virtue remains unassailed; the Child is the Saviour through whose goodness erring adults find redemption. Translated to the cinema we find the child heroes of Italian films are constantly shown as revealing to grown-ups the

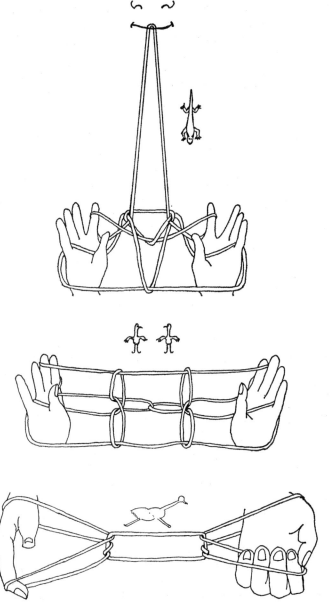

48 Australian aborigines' string figures. (*a*) Crocodile, (*b*) two cocka-
toos, (*c*) an emu.

wickedness of adult lives. Often, as in *The White Line*, the child dies and it is over his corpse or grave that the corrupt adults repent and are reconciled. In *Bicycle Thieves* a father is brought face to face with his own ignominy when his devoted little son sees him steal a bicycle. In *Miracle of Milan* the innate goodness of a young orphan eventually brings a squatters' camp of down-and-out good-for-nothings to a state of salvation in which they are transported behind him into the celestial world which opens to receive them above Milan cathedral. In *His Last Twelve Hours* a dead father condemned to eternal damnation returns to earth where his daughter prompts him to one generous act which he believes will seal his fate. In fact it proves to be his redemption.

In these films, unlike British or American ones, the young inexperienced virgin always wins out over her more experienced and seductive rivals.

In English films the outstanding theme may be summed up as: 'Is the adult worthy of the child's trust?' Moral issues take a prominent place. The children put implicit trust in some adult. The adult is sensitively aware of this and will often renounce an ambition, confess to a crime or suffer punishment rather than betray the child's trust. The theme of misunderstanding is common, in which one of these trusting children is led to believe that his idolized adult is guilty of a crime which he has not committed. Aspects of these relationships are well shown in *The Browning Version*, *The Spanish Gardener*, *Tiger Bay*, *Whistle Down the Wind*, *The Fallen Idol* and *Personal Affair*.

It is only in British films that adults are shown in the image of a perfect father figure.

In American films the father of a child is not a hero: he normally has a kind of playmate or elder brother role. The child's 'ideal man', who is strong, resourceful, brave, honest, independent and chivalrous, must come from afar, as in *Shane* or *The Rainmaker*. Alternatively the child must go far to find him, as in *The Little Fugitive*.

In modern American life, where children are expected and encouraged to surpass their fathers, they must turn to other men in their search for a masculine ideal. Hence we find the great emphasis which these films give to cowboys, virtuous gun-fighters, noble Indians, G.I. heroes and other super-figures.

These few examples from a modern art medium illustrate the

close relationship between any art and the attitudes of the society which practises it.

In recent European history the great artistic geniuses stand out like beacons amid the average men. Giotto, Rubens, Cézanne, Mozart, Henry Moore, Nijinsky, Racine and Lope de Vega are names whose equals number only a few dozen out of all the hundreds of millions who have lived in Europe during the past millenium. In other words, with us creative ability is rare. Even to practise art, however indifferently, is far from universal in modern English society when once the compulsion of school is ended although many persons seek some modest artistic expression in such activities as embroidery, Scottish or ballroom dancing, music-making, garden design, flower arrangement or cookery.

Primitive tribes are quite different. As a rule everyone in the group will learn one or several arts. All Eskimo women learn to embellish clothing to a degree of beauty far beyond any demands made by the weather. From an early age all Yakut girls of Siberia or Pomo and Maidu of California weave the incredibly neat and beautiful baskets that are the highest development of their tribal art (Fig. 44). No one is artistically indifferent or idle as they often are with us. Everyone joins in to the best of his ability, which must be one of the reasons why the average standard of creative work is so extremely high. In such circumstances startling advances do not come from a rare Brunelleschi or Beethoven, they happen all the time as a result of numberless little innovations from innumerable nameless people. In a primitive tribe everyone is an artist.

Some writers make a distinction here and say that the embellishment of tools, weapons and clothing – that is decorative art – is the work of artisans, not artists. The discrimination seems unreal. Pottery may range from the crude shapes of Bronze Age cremation urns with a few notches cut into them to the magnificence of the finest Greek or Chinese vases. At what stage along this progression does the artisan become the artist?

Decoration may be chiefly concentrated on shape and design, without concerning itself to express ideas or to portray objects. This is *formal* decoration. It is seen in the elegant shaping of a wooden bowl or in the pottery impressed with finely toothed stamps of the Beaker people. Formal designs of this sort add nothing to the functional efficiency of the object; they serve to

49 Wooden figurine. Fang reliquary. West Africa. Height 16¾ in.

50 Painting from a Kwakiutl house front. It represents a killer whale
(After Boas.)

release emotions and feelings which may otherwise find no
expression.

Other designs may portray a real object, a person, animal, plant
or imaginary scene. This is *representative* decoration. If it closely
portrays the original model it is termed naturalistic; when far
from it, stylized. Figure 49 shows an African figurine of Fang
workmanship from the Congo. It is clearly naturalistic. By
contrast, Figure 50 shows a painting from the house front of a
Kwakiutl village. American North-west Coast art is amongst the
most stylized that can be found. This painting represents a killer

whale. The animal has been split along its whole back towards the front. The two profiles of the head are joined, with the mouth below, which is flanked by gills (biologically unreal but symbolizing a water animal). The dorsal fin is placed above the head. The flippers flank the two sides of the body, whilst the two halves of the tail are turned outwards so as to form a straight line above the square doorway of the house. It is a sophisticated art which fuses, with great ingenuity, the Kwakiutl hunter's interest in animal anatomy, his impulse towards design, his dislike of blank spaces and his totemic mythology.

This North-west Coast art seems to have derived its fantastic complexity from (a) superb technical mastery of its materials, (b) an elaborately stratified social organization in which descent from mythological ancestors is emphasized, (c) the translation of ritual dance dramas into the plastic arts and (d) an unusually intense need to externalize emotional drives. It is an art which reveals totally different values from the fetish shown in Figure 49.

Here, as in much of African carving, mass, solidity, the junction of planes and plainess of surface are the artist's goals. He is limited by the toughness of his wood and by the small scale of the block from which he carves. Hence, his figures have disproportionately large heads, their arms are kept tucked close to the body, legs are reduced in size or shown in a crouched position, the end result tends to be vertically linear and compact, giving a basic generalization of the body without fussy decorative additions. But what, above all, integrates so many of these figures into the most tenaciously held values of the African's culture is their role as fetishes. They house the spirits of ancestors and are awful with superhuman power. Their form is human but a god dwells within. As always, the form, content and significance of this art is tightly organized into the basic postulates of their cultural system.

We have already said something about the range of arts which may be practised by different societies. Song, dance and 'oral literature' are universal. So, too, is some kind of plastic art. What we need to stress is that among most peoples there is no gulf between art and the ordinary practical jobs of life. Ordinary jobs are done as artistically as possible. If a Solomon Islander wants a canoe paddle he carves an elegant pattern on it; a Pawnee buffalo-hide tent or *tipi*, to use the Dakota name (*wigwam* is the Algonkin word for a bark-covered house), is adorned with paintings;

Fijian bark cloth will have geometric designs woven into it; Arapaho, Cheyenne or Sioux moccasins are made with 'heraldic' embellishments, a Mehinacu stool may be carved to look like a puma (Fig. 31).

In general we can say that the arts practised by any group of people will be those related to the crafts most useful to them. Whether these are chasing metal, carving wood, painting pots or weaving baskets will depend on the culture pattern of the group. Sometimes the most highly developed art may be related not to a craft but to some other form of behaviour. Dancing and drama are often of supreme importance in religious rituals. We find this in the Zuni and Hopi Pueblo Indians. With us drama is seldom employed in this way, although it used to be in the Mystery and Miracle plays of the Middle Ages. It survives today in such self-conscious displays as the performance of the Oberammergau passion.

When we turn to consider the function of art we find that different arts serve different purposes and the same art may be used in quite distinct ways by different tribes. Basically, the practice of any art serves to release tensions within the subconscious mind and to enable the artist to 'unload' or externalize his pent-up emotions and ideas. This release of tension brings pleasure and a sense of relief or well being to the artist, whilst the people who see what he has done share his enjoyment in their role of critic or admirer. It is a form of communication and serves as yet another of the forces which bind society, although we know so little about the physiology of emotion that it is difficult to say exactly how it works. From the individual and his immediate group the effects of art spread widely into many aspects of society and culture. In some cultures the arts are used to give precise and profound expression to their most cherished and basic institutions or assumptions. Medieval religious beliefs were made explicit in painting, architecture, stained glass and much else. At other times artists may attack and seek to destroy what they believe to be false or evil in their culture, as the Dadaists did about 1920.

People often devote a great deal of time and effort to making a pot, shield, house gable or garment into a superb work of art without in any way improving its practical efficiency. This implies that the gratification of an artistic need – or artistic self-expression – gives a deep sense of satisfaction to many people. A task beauti-

fully done rewards them also with the admiration of their neighbours. It has prestige value, that most sought-after of all human
goals. This seems to be a basic drive which underlies the practice
of any art.

In most tribes the artists will all be creating the same kind of art,
such as cedarwood boxes among the Tlingit, Chilkat blankets,
Mochica pottery (Plate XIII), Benin bronzes, Semang combs (Fig.
27), Maori tattooing, Bushman shell beads and so on. This gives
a sense of tribal identity. As a psychologist would say, it reinforces
the feeling of belonging to the *in-group*. It is one more way in
which social solidarity and security are developed. This is especially the case where neighbouring and closely related tribes
emphasize their separateness from one another and their own
identity by using different designs on similar objects: different
face painting, moccasin patterns or pot shapes for example.
Another aspect of this is found in the art of oral literature, in which
tribal artists often recite long and intricately devised tales or poems
recounting the origin, mythology and legends of their people. This
sets them securely apart from neighbours who have different
legends.

Many peoples have devised riddles, proverbs or fables that play
an important part in teaching children, in enshrining tribal
wisdom or in inculcating moral principles (Plate XIV).

Other forms of art are used in magic rituals. It is likely that the
Stone Age cave paintings were connected with hunting magic to
make the bison, reindeer and horses plentiful and easy to kill.

To sum up, we can say that the art of every people, like all else
in their cultures, is closely organized and integrated into the total
pattern of their social life. It is part of the many ways in which
human relationships are kept jogging along with tolerable smooth-
ness and a minimum of ill-feeling or disruption. Most people get a
feeling of pleasure, of 'life enhancement', when they see or hear a
work of art. So almost any such work, especially among primitives,
helps to unite the group and make people feel well disposed
towards each other.

Only in our own Western society, which is largely indifferent to
the arts, do people become violently hostile to a genius such as
Picasso because he invents cubism or Schönberg when he com-
poses in a twelve-tone scale.

12 MODERN SOCIETIES

Modern societies and the uses of anthropology

The ethnographic present, modern societies,
applied anthropology, a question of conscience,
anthropology and the future.

Much of this book has been about the customs of primitive tribes. This is not because they are any more – or any less – important to anthropologists than the advanced European and American civilizations.

The study of primitives greatly occupies anthropologists for the simple reason that if it is not pursued now with speed and urgency there will soon be no tribal cultures left to study. Either the primitives themselves will have become extinct, like the native Tasmanians, or they will have changed their social identity through *acculturation*, to a more or less complete adoption of a European way of life.

Already this process has gone much further than might be supposed from reading this book.

In discussing tribal customs we have often used what is known as the *ethnographic present*. This is a conventional way of speaking in the present tense about past events and circumstances. The 'ethnographic present' for any people is the date when they were first exposed to the impact of a Western type of culture. For the Aztecs this would be about A.D. 1519, the year Cortez arrived; for the Wampanoag Indians of Massachusetts 1620, the year of the *Mayflower*'s landfall; for the Hawaiians 1778, the time of their rediscovery by Captain Cook; and for some of the remoter tribes of New Guinea it would only be within the last five or ten years.

A result of using the ethnographic present is that in speaking of a primitive people, the Eskimo for example, we have said 'They do so-and-so . . .' meaning 'They did it when first observed by Europeans or modern Americans; it was their traditional way of life' – which may or may not be their practice today. In fact, a few Eskimo groups continue to follow their traditional culture fairly closely. Most of them have been greatly modified by acculturation. They have adopted rifles for hunting, metal tools, canned food, mail-order furniture and many other European traits. And in

1967, Mr. Noah Carpenter, of Banks Island, North West Territories, who already holds the degree of B.Sc., was accepted by the University of Manitoba as the first Eskimo ever to win a place in a Canadian medical school. Changes of this sort are taking place all over the world. In 1970 one of the most promising young tennis players in Australia is a charming and elegant girl named Evonne Goolagong. She also happens to be an aborigine (Plate XVI).

In other words it must be remembered that changes may have occurred (or will occur this year or next) in many of the customs that we have described according to their traditional pattern.

For a long time anthropologists paid little attention to analysing their own modern American or European societies. Those days are past. All aspects of current society and culture are now being explored by anthropological techniques. Advanced political and social systems, scientific methodology, economic cause and effect, mass psychology, the relationship between management and workers in industry, the handling of international affairs, problems of racism, the causes of crime and the requirements of space travel are only a few of the affairs in which anthropologists are making valuable contributions to knowledge. These contributions offer the prospect of bringing increased stability into human relationships and promote the psychological security that goes with it.

Governments and other political powers can be surprisingly stupid in handling cross-cultural situations, even when they mean well. Values such as 'decent Christian behaviour' or 'democratic fairness' may annoy, rather than allure, when urged upon a Moslem dictatorship, as happened at a critical phase of World War II.

In the past, missionaries have sometimes been surprised or resentful when they found that, despite their cajoling efforts, a tribe resisted the particular brand of Methodism or Anglicanism to which they were trying to convert it. This may merely have been due to the fact that the natives were a matriarchal, matrilineal group who worshipped, and perhaps traced their origin from, a mother goddess. It follows that they would not easily accept the dominance of God the Father and God the Son. If they had been offered Roman Catholicism, the cult of the Virgin Mary might have been immediately intelligible and acceptable to them.

Commercial firms may complain that they cannot get the natives in some remote district to work for them, in spite of increasing inducements of money or goods. An anthropologist might suspect that the natives' hesitation was because they were inhibited by dangerous taboos, or felt themselves to be lacking in some magic ritual necessary for the task, or were simply uninterested in the value system upon which European motivations are based.

In factories, it is common to see persons sitting at their machines in awkward positions, or standing when they could be sitting, or complaining of aching arms and backs at the end of the day. A physical anthropologist would at once guess that the machines were designed by engineers who knew little of the needs and abilities of the human body. He would see how the lay-out of the controls could be improved so that a worker sitting comfortably and relaxed could reach, without effort, any knobs and levers he had to handle. In these situations tiring eye movements should be eliminated; the required sequence of actions should be one that comes easily to human muscles and joints; physical factors remote from the body yet greatly affecting it, such as noise, lighting, temperature and much else, should all be carefully controlled. In factories where attention is given to details of this kind, production is likely to be high and absenteeism rare, provided that the social setting is equally well organized.

These simple examples show how anthropology can help people to understand each other, to avoid giving offence even whilst they seek to please and to ensure the most relaxed situations for us all.

But they raise questions of fundamental importance for every anthropologist: *ought* he to take part in any attempt to influence social or political situations? Ought he, if consulted by a government or some organization however well meaning, to give advice about how to handle a problem concerning primitive or tribal societies? Should he, in fact, become a consultant and accept clients? Most anthropologists have been extremely wary in the face of these questions; many have a strong aversion from committing themselves to advice or action on behalf of dominant groups. Governments and international organizations are normally concerned to govern and to organize simpler peoples according to an administrative programme which is often little related to the needs or wishes of the persons who are being governed. An anthropologist, though theoretically neutral, tends to see problems and difficulties from the point of view of the primitives. It is often impossible to help without becoming political and he usually prefers not to become immersed in these muddy waters. He is a scientist and scholar who acknowledges only one master: the truth as he learns it. There are, of course, exceptions. An anthropologist is a citizen – of his own country and of the world. Many are ready to put the knowledge they have derived from the study of man to the service of man. But it is far easier to talk of doing this than to carry it into effect. To practice what is called *applied anthropology* often calls for a deep and heart-searching look into one's conscience. Only if our professional and scientific integrity can be seen to emerge clear and unblemished is it proper to accept the ultimate responsibility of proceeding from investigation to action.

This means that, in general and with few exceptions, anthropology will be of most use to mankind in proportion as it avoids direct meddling in human affairs. Let it pursue its humanistic purpose with its scientific techniques; let it find the truth and teach the truth. But, at least until 'action anthropology' has been more fully tried, let it avoid the entanglement and dangers of playing the power game, in whatever guise. It is for the presidents, politicians, administrators, committees, economists, and governors to arrange the affairs of social groups. It is also their responsibility to heed the truths which any science, including anthropology, may reveal.

Few persons have a professional training in anthropology but everyone can develop something of the anthropologist's attitude towards other people, their problems and endeavours. All we need is to realize that the habits and customs of our own society are not the only way to do things nor, perhaps, even the best way. Many societies have found quite different solutions to the problems which we, and all groups, have to face. We must be sympathetic to their efforts and behaviour, seeking to learn what they can teach rather than to force our ideas on them; assessing them by their own values, not ours.

If we ask: What has anthropology to offer ordinary men and women going about the everyday affairs of our society?, it is precisely in its power to change their outlook that we may find the answer. All around us tension, animosity and uncertainty prevail, as new culture traits arise to modify our own lives in one direction, those of our neighbours in another. Today's world of supermarkets, Coronation Street, rising criminality, drug dependence, planned obsolescence and largely unplanned leisure offers a pitfall and a challenge to us all. The pitfall is a smug satisfaction with our own rectitude, a conviction of the infallibility of our judgements and opinion. The challenge is how to emerge from the comfort of this hide-bound self-esteem to an awareness of other viewpoints. If we are intolerant of the Joneses because they 'waste' six nights a week at bingo or roulette, of the Smiths who seem obsessed with the performance of dozens of football teams, and of the Robinsons who were sexually promiscuous before their marriage and casually permissive after it, anthropology may deepen our perspective. It may remind us that the Thai and Alorese are enthusiastic gamblers, that Zuni is obsessed with minute details of its endless ritual dancing, and that many peoples throughout the world have been far more sexually 'permissive' than we are. It may further remind us that all these societies have functioned – in terms of human companionship and human happiness – at least as efficiently as ours. If there are more ways than one of killing a cat, there are also more ways than one of bringing richness and pleasure to its life.

It is not the task of an anthropologist to prescribe sexual permissiveness for us because the Samoans have practised it, nor to oppose it because the Manus are prudish, coy and puritanical. But, by showing how other peoples have behaved in comparable situations, he can give us a clearer view of our own problems and a rational, rather than emotional, basis for our response to them. He can analyse a social phenomenon, display it in its relative world context and reveal something about how it correlates with our different reactions to it.

Anthropology, perhaps more than most disciplines, is based on a vast body of facts which, to be understood, must be seen in an integrated and meaningful relationship. But it is far more than this. For an anthropologist it is a way of life, a set of values, a torch to illumine his path and to hand on to others. But no anthropologist wants to decree how other people shall think and behave. They must still form their own judgements and remain responsible for their own acts.

Sixty million years ago a tiny tree shrew, the earliest of all the Primates, began the upward evolution that was to end in man. Some animals – the coelacanth is a well-known one – have existed through many millions of years and long geological epochs. Perhaps man, too, avoiding self-destruction by a hair's breadth, will survive for another ten or twenty million years as the noblest species of terrestrial life.

We can hardly begin to imagine what marvels and inventions he will have compassed by then, nor what splendid expeditions through space and time will be his destiny. But we can perhaps be certain that before these lofty ventures are attained he must, at long last, have found the way to live in peace and unity with all his neighbours. If he fails in this he may have little future left.

There is no magic charm or incantation to make real the dream of future peace on earth but anthropology, beyond all studies, is the most likely to teach the brotherhood of races and the love of man for men.

APPENDICES

Appendix A

Suggestions for further reading

ARENSBERG, C. M. 1959. *Family and community in Ireland*. Gloucester, Mass.: P. Smith.

BENEDICT, Ruth. 1946. *The chrysanthemum and the sword*. Boston: Houghton Mifflin. London: Routledge. This may be read in conjunction with the book by Sugimoto (q.v.).

BOWEN, Elenore Smith. 1956. *Return to laughter*. London: Gollancz. A (pseudonymous) account of life in an African tribe and what field work means to an anthropologist.

BRIDGES, E. Lucas. 1948. *Uttermost part of the earth*. London: Hodder and Stoughton. An autobiographical account of life among the natives of Tierra del Fuego.

BUCK, Sir Peter H. 1950. *The Coming of the Maori*. 2nd ed. Wellington, N.Z.: Whitcombe and Tombs. Sir Peter H. Buck is the English name of the distinguished Maori writer Te Rangi Hiroa.

COMAS, Juan. 1960. *Manual of physical anthropology*. Springfield, Ill.: Thomas. A useful introduction to the subject.

EISELEY, Loren C. 1959. *The immense journey*. New York: Modern Library. (Modern Library of the World's Best Books, P47.)

EVANS-PRITCHARD, E. E. 1940. *The Nuer, a description of the modes of livelihood and political institutions of a Nilotic people*. Oxford: Clarendon Press.

FINLEY, M. I. 1956. *The world of Odysseus*. London: Chatto and Windus. This is an attempt by a classical scholar to reconstruct the life of ancient Greece from the evidence of heroic poetry.

FORDE, C. Daryll. 1934. *Habitat, economy and society*. London: Methuen. A splendid introduction to the subject.

GLADWIN, Thomas, and SARASON, S. B. 1953. *Truk: man in paradise*. New York: Wenner-Gren Foundation for Anthropological Research.

GOLDING, William. 1955. *The inheritors*. London: Faber and Faber. An imaginative reconstruction of family life and racial conflict in the Old Stone Age, by the novelist author of *Lord of the Flies*.

HAMMOND, Peter B. 1969. *Cultural and social anthropology: an introduction*. New York: Macmillan.

HANNERZ, Ulf. 1969. *Soulside. Inquiries into ghetto culture and community*. New York: Columbia University Press.

HOEBEL, E. A. 1958. *Man in the primitive world; an introduction to anthropology*. 2nd ed. New York: McGraw Hill.

JENNESS, Diamond. 1959. *People of the twilight*. Chicago: University Chicago Press. An excellent popular account of Eskimo life.

KLUCKHOHN, Clyde. 1950. *Mirror for man*. London: Harrap. How an anthropologist sees his subject in relation to modern life.

KROEBER, A. L. 1948. *Anthropology: race, language, culture, psychology, prehistory*. London: Harrap. The revised edition of a standard textbook; it still has much to recommend it despite the time that has elapsed since its publication.

KROEBER, Theodora. 1961. *Ishi in two worlds*. Berkeley and Los Angeles: University California Press. A remarkable story of the last wild Indian (a Yahi) to survive in the United States, and his life among modern Americans.

LÉVI-STRAUSS, C. 1961. *A world on the wane*. London: Hutchinson. This is a slightly shortened version of *Tristes tropiques*, a beautifully written account of life among the natives of the Amazonian region.

LIN YUTANG. 1936. *My country and my people*. London: Heinemann.

LIPS, Julius E. 1949. *The origin of things*. London: Harrap. Easy reading, many illustrations, extensive book list. Suitable for young readers.

LOWIE, Robert H. 1956. *The Crow Indians*. New York: Rinehart.

LYND, Robert S. and Helen M. 1959. *Middletown, a study in American culture*. New York: Harcourt, Brace. London: Constable.

MALINOWSKI, Bronislaw. 1935. *Coral gardens and their magic*. London: Allen and Unwin.

MEAD, Margaret. 1949. *Male and female, a study of the sexes in a changing world*. New York: Morrow. London: Penguin.

MEAD, Margaret, and WOLFENSTEIN, M. (Eds.). 1955. *Childhood in contemporary cultures*. Chicago: Chicago University Press.

OAKLEY, K. P. 1950. *Man the toolmaker*. London: British Museum. A useful introduction to Stone Age cultures.

PIDDINGTON, R. 1950/1957. *An introduction to social anthropology*. Edinburgh: Oliver and Boyd. 2 vols.

PITT-RIVERS, Julian A. 1954. *The people of the Sierra*. London: Weidenfeld and Nicolson. An account of life in a Spanish town.

POWDERMAKER, Hortense. 1950. *Hollywood, the dream factory*. Boston: Little, Brown. An anthropologist looks at the movie-makers.

RADCLIFFE-BROWN, A. R., and FORDE, C. D. (eds.) 1950. *African systems of kinship and marriage*. London: Oxford University Press.
RADIN, Paul (Ed.). 1960. *Autobiography of a Winnebago Indian*. New York: Dover. London: Constable. First published in 1920 under the title: *Crashing Thunder; the autobiography of an American Indian*. An anthropological classic.
RICHARDS, Audrey I. 1939. *Land, labour and diet in Northern Rhodesia; an economic study of the Bemba tribe*. London: Oxford University Press.

SCHLAUCH, Margaret. 1955. *The gift of language*. New York: Dover. London: Constable. A good introduction to the study of language.
SPENCER, Baldwin, and GILLEN, F. J. 1912. *Across Australia*. London: Macmillan. One of the early classics of anthropology.
SUGIMOTO, E. I. 1933. *A daughter of the Samurai*. London: Hutchinson. The autobiography of a Japanese lady.
SUMNER, W. G. 1959. *Folkways*. New York: Dover. London: Constable. First published in 1906, this is a pioneer text in the study of social behaviour, manners, customs and morals. Extremely readable.

WELLS, Calvin. 1964. *Bones, bodies and disease*. London: Thames and Hudson. Especially written for easy reading; good illustrations; bibliography.
WISSLER, Clark. 1950. *The American Indian*. 3rd ed. New York: Peter Smith. First published in 1917. Still a useful general survey.

Unlike physicians, lawyers or clergymen, who have a long professional ancestry, trained anthropologists are a product of only the last two generations. Many enquiring travellers, like Herodotus and Marco Polo, were fascinated by exotic peoples or customs and wrote ethnographical descriptions of them but until recently anthropology was studied only by men who had been trained in other subjects. These included medicine (W. H. R. Rivers and C. G. Seligman), biology (Baldwin Spencer and A. C. Haddon), psychology (C. S. Myers), sociology (W. G. Sumner), classics (J. G. Frazer), anatomy (G. Elliot Smith and Arthur Keith) and much else.

Some of the older volumes in the above list reflect this diversity of approach. A few are by writers with no training in anthropology or any related subject, yet make useful background reading. *A daughter of the Samurai* is one of these. Several of these books exist in more than the one edition listed and may be published by different houses.

M

Appendix B

Anthropological films

Catalogues of films of anthropological interest are available from (*a*) The Audio-Visual Center, Indiana University, Indiana, U.S.A., and (*b*) The Audio-Visual Aids Library, Pennsylvania State University, Pennsylvania, U.S.A.

The following brief selection of films will cater for varied tastes. They are a very small selection out of the large number available and vary greatly in standard, both anthropologically and photographically. All of them are suitable for non-specialist audiences.

1. *Nanook of the North.* (1920/21) After 50 years Robert Flaherty's great classic still remains a wonderful film of the life of an Eskimo hunter.

2. *One hundred years of archaeology in India.* Produced by the Government of India. (1962) 16 mm. black-and-white, optical sound. 18 minutes. Available from The Information Service of India, 2107 Massachusetts Avenue, N.W. Washington 8, D.C.

3. *Dead Birds.* Filmed and produced by Robert Gardner. 16 mm. colour, optical sound. 83 minutes. From Contemporary Films, Inc., 267 West 25th Street, New York, N.Y.
Shows life in the Dani tribe of New Guinea. A prize winning film.

4. *Benin Kingship Rituals.* Filmed 1959/60 by Francis Speed. 16 mm. colour, optical sound. 25 minutes. From Francis Speed, University of Ibadan.
A festival of traditional arts, drama and costume. Rich in music of the Bini people.

5a. *Dream dances of the Kashia Pomo.* (1963) 16 mm. colour, optical sound. 30 minutes; and
5b. *Pomo shaman.* (1963) 16 mm. black-and-white, optical sound. 20 minutes. From Film Sales Department, University of California Extension Media Center, 2223 Fulton Street, Berkeley, California 94720.
Both these films show aspects of life in a tribe of American Indians.

6. *The Land Dayaks of Borneo.* (1961/66) Filmed by William R. Geddes. 16 mm. colour, optical sound. 38 minutes. From New York University Film Library, 26 Washington Place, New York, N.Y. 10003. A vivid and informative film.

7. *Excavations at La Venta.* (1963) 16 mm. colour, optical sound. 29 minutes. From the University of California Extension Media Center, 2223 Fulton Street, Berkeley, California 94720.

Records 3 seasons of field work at a great ceremonial site of the early Olmec civilization, Mexico.

8. *Netsilik Eskimo fishing at the Stone Weir.* (1963) 16 mm. colour, silent. 57½ minutes. From Film Librarian, Educational Services, Inc., 47 Galen Street, Watertown, Mass. 02172.

9. *Chinese, Korean and Japanese Dance.* (1964/5) 16 mm. colour, optical sound. 28 minutes. From Sales and Rental Unit, Bureau of Audio-Visual Instruction, 131 Livingston Street, Brooklyn, New York, N.Y. 11201.

This film was designed especially for school children.

10. *Circle of the Sun.* (1960) Produced by the National Film Board of Canada. 16 mm. colour, optical sound. 30 minutes. From Contemporary Films Inc., 267 West 25th Street, New York, N.Y. 10001.

A record of the Blood Indians, one of the three Blackfoot tribes. Despite its title it does not show the annual sun dance of the tribe. High standard of filming technique.

11. *Totem Pole.* (1963) 16 mm. colour, optical sound. 27 minutes. From University of California Extension Media Center, 2223 Fulton Street, Berkeley, California 94720.

On totem poles and wood carving, chiefly from the Kwakiutl tribe of British Columbia, Canada.

12a. *Acorns: the staple food of the California Indians.* (1962) 28 minutes.
12b. *Buckeyes: a food of the California Indians.* (1961) 13 minutes.
12c. *Pine nuts: a food of the Paiute and Washo Indians.* 13 minutes.

All 16 mm. colour, optical sound. From University of California Extension Media Center, 2223 Fulton Street, Berkeley, California 94720.

All show details of the gathering and preparation of traditional native foods.

13. *Matjemosh.* (1964) Filmed by A. A. Gerbrands, Rijksmuseum voor Volkenkunde, Leiden, Netherlands. 16 mm. colour, optical sound. 27 minutes. From Universitaire Film, Utrecht.

Matjemosh is a wood carver in the village of Amanamkai, New Guinea. The film is about his art.

14. *The Exiles.* (1959/61) 16 mm. optical sound. 72 minutes. From Contemporary Films, Inc., 267 West 25th Street, New York, N.Y.

10001. A great documentary film. It shows a group of young American Indians trying to adapt to an alien way of life – modern urban Los Angeles.

15. *Amazon Family.* (1961) 16 mm. colour, optical sound. 19 minutes. From International Film Foundation, 475 Fifth Avenue, New York, N.Y. 10017.
The life of a rubber collector in Peru.

16. *The Ancient Egyptian.* Produced by Julian Bryan. 16 mm. colour, optical sound. 27 minutes. From International Film Foundation, 475 Fifth Avenue, New York, N.Y. 10017. One of the best ever films on ancient Old World cultures.

17. *The Loon's Necklace.* A fine film on masks of the North-west Coast American Indians.

Appendix C

A few museums which contain material of anthropological (ethnographical) interest

Birmingham City Museum, Congreve Street, Birmingham, 3.

British Museum, Great Russell Street, London, W.C.1.

University Museum of Archaeology and Ethnology, Downing Street, Cambridge.

City of Glasgow Corporation Art Gallery and Museum, Kelvingrove, Glasgow.

The University of Newcastle-upon-Tyne, Department of Anthropology, 11 Sydenham Terrace, Newcastle-upon-Tyne.

The Pitt-Rivers Museum, Parks Road, Oxford.

Extensive archaeological collections are held by these and many other museums. See the annual index publication *Museums and Galleries in Great Britain and Ireland.* Index Publishers, 69 Victoria Street, London, S.W.1.

Appendix D

Useful addresses

The Commonwealth Institute, Kensington High Street, London, W.8. Tel: 01–937 8252.

The International African Institute, 10 Fetter Lane, London, E.C.4. Tel: 01–353 4751.

The National Film Archive, 81 Dean Street, London, W.1. Tel: 01–437 4355.

The Royal Anthropological Institute, 21 Bedford Square, London, W.C.1. Tel: 01–636 2980.

The Society for the Study of Human Biology (General Secretary Dr. W. A. Marshall), The University of London Institute of Child Health, Great Ormond Street, London, W.C.1. Tel: 01–405 9200.

INDEX